Christian Response to Human Trafficking

Christian Response to Human Trafficking

Biblical, Theological, Ethical, Ministerial, NGOs, and Legal Perspectives

Edited by
Sangtemkala

Clark Centre for Peace Research and Action (CCPRA)
Clark Theological College

&

Christian World Imprints

CCPRA Publication Series No. 11

First Published in 2020 by

Clark Centre for Peace Research and Action (CCPRA)
Clark Theological College
Aolijen, Mokokchung 798601 / Nagaland
ctcprin@gmail.com
www.ctcnagaland.com
Phone: 09436006979

&

Christian World Imprints
Christian Publishing & Books from India
C-3, Wazirpur Industrial Area
Delhi-110052
cwidelhi2017@gmail.com
www.ChristianWorldImprints.com
Phone: +91 11 41526079

ISBN: 978-93-5148-432-5 (HB)
ISBN: 978-93-5148-433-2 (PB)

Printed in India.

Contents

Foreword

Living together in peace with one another is the most desired aspiration and of paramount importance for each person in the society. Peace can be disturbed and taken away when the evils of society, like human trafficking, creeps in and operates in the society which especially victimizes and exploits the women, children and weaker sections of the people in the society. According to the United Nations, human trafficking is defined as "The recruitment, transportation, transfer, harboring, or receipt of persons, by means of the threat or use of force or other forms of coercion, of abduction, of fraud, of deception, of the abuse of power or of a position of vulnerability or of the giving or receiving of payment or benefits to achieve the consent of a person having control over another person, for the purpose of exploitation."[1] In fact, human trafficking is a crime and offense which cogently exploits and abuses men, women, children and poor people for commercial purpose. According to report, human trafficking earns global profits of approximately $150 billion a year for traffickers, $ 99 billion of which comes from commercial sexual exploitation.[2] Human trafficking can be seen as modern slavery. Globally, it is estimated that 71% of enslaved people are women and girls, while the remaining 29% are men and boys.[3] Also, research shows that the mass majority of cases of human trafficking go on undetected because either the cases of trafficking are not reported or distorted.

---

1 https://www. nij.gov>crime>pages accessed on 10-01-2020.

2 "Human Trafficking by the numbers." Human Rights First. Accessed 10-01-2020. https://www.Humanrightsfirst.org/resource/human-trafficking-numbers.

3 "Trafficking and Slavery Fact Sheet." Free the Slave. Accessed on 10-01-2020. https://www.freetheslaves.net/wep-content/uploads/2018/04/Trafficking-ans-Slavery-Fact-Sheet-April-2018. pdf.

In India, in general and in Northeast India particularly, there is a high demand for domestic help, cheap labour, and sex workers in urban and commercial sectors that provide opportunity for human trafficking. As a result, many innocent people are being exploited and victimized which bring serious concerns to the church and society.

In view of this present scenario of human trafficking in the society and to address the issues from different perspectives, the Clark Centre for Peace Research and Action (CCPRA) has timely organized the seminar on November 16-18, 2017, on the theme: *Human Trafficking: The Dehumanizing Reality*. The articles contributed by different scholars from the biblical, theological, legal, ethical and ministerial perspectives will enable the readers to see the dehumanizing reality of human trafficking in the society, which is a global as well as local issue. In addition, it will provide space to give an apt response to human trafficking by engaging in terms of dealing with the prevention of trafficking in person, protection of victims of human trafficking and prosecution of trafficking offenders. As a result, it may have a positive impact in the lives of many of the victims of human trafficking by experiencing peace, justice and human dignity. I would like to express my sincere appreciation to Dr. Sangtemkala for taking the trouble of editing this volume. In this connection, I want to thank Miss Imtiwala Imchen, Programme Coordinator, CCPRA, for putting in a lot of effort to bring out this book for readership. I hope that this volume will be a channel of peace for many people in the society who need our attention and support.

Rev. Dr. A. Temjen Jamir
Academic Dean
Clark Theological College

Acknowledgements

At the outset, I express my sincere thanks to the members of the CCPRA committee, CTC, for giving me the honour to edit this book on behalf of the Committee. I am also grateful to Rev. Dr. Marnungsang, the Principal and the Advisor to CCPRA for all his support for yet another publication of the Centre. Secondly, I am also grateful to Rev. Dr. A. Temjen Jamir for writing the foreword for this volume.

Thirdly, I acknowledge with thanks the hard works of all the paper writers for taking all the pains in writing, presenting and willingly sending in their papers to be included in this volume.

Fourthly, on behalf of the CCPRA I would like to record our profound gratitude for the continued support of the Evangelisches Missionswerk in Deutschland (EMW, Germany) for the ongoing activities of the CCPRA for the promotion of peace and justice. May God continue to bless and prosper their efforts to propagate the Gospel around the world.

Fifthly, I also would like to acknowledge the tireless works and persuasive initiatives of Miss Imtiwala Imchen, the Co-ordinator of the CCPRA for initiating and organizing all the programmes of the Centre and seeing through that everything is brought to its logical conclusion including this publication.

Finally, our words are not enough to express our gratitude again to the Christian World Imprints (CWI), Delhi for their ever willingness to help us with efficient work and generous partnership with the CCPRA and for seeing through all the stages of this publication with keen interest.

The Editor

Introduction

A Backdrop Note

Human trafficking is one of the most heinous crimes that has relentlessly violated the very essence of being human. As such, this is a pressing challenge to the global human community's peaceful and meaningful co-existence. This criminal activity diminishes, destroys, and violates human rights, human dignity, and shatters the total life of individuals and communities both at the micro and macro levels across all limits. It is the second most 'profitable' criminal activity (if there is any meaningful profit for any one for that matter) with a tune of a gross eight billion U.S. dollars a year and constantly expanding and multiplying that grows within and beyond all limits of boundaries and borders.

In order to address and initiate various responses to this challenging issue and related problems, a National Seminar on the theme: 'Human Trafficking: The Dehumanizing Reality', was organized by the Clark Centre for Peace and Research Action of the Clark Theological College, which was held from 16-18, November 2017 at Aolijen, Mokokchung, Nagaland. The papers in this volume were presented at that Seminar. They represent a wide range of lived experiences and expertise that directly deal with questions such as, what is human trafficking, what are the root causes and effects, who and what does it involve, and perhaps most importantly, how should we as Church, institutions, organizations and Christians respond to this variegated crime commonly called the modern slavery?

Highlights of the Chapters

The *Keynote Address* by Asha Sanchu traces human trafficking as far back as the Joseph story which could be the first trafficked man in the Bible. Then, in the *first chapter* she argues that women and young girls are the most vulnerable targeted victims of human trafficking in the North East India which is the result of all the evils of gender inequality in our society. This evil is further accentuated by the factors of protracted political unrest across the interstate and international borders which is then abetted and aggravated by economic instability, and the ever growing depression and anxiety over the problem of unemployment and better opportunities for healthy and meaningful life.

In the *second chapter*, T. Chubayanger deals with prevalence of trafficking associated with child labour in our region from a legal point of view. His paper supplies various Homes and Centres as well as some helpful statistics on the problems of human trafficking. He argues that despite various international conventions, constitutional and legal provisions and acts for prevention and protection of children at risk the criminal acts of child and young people trafficking continues unabated in our region due to ever increasing migrations from economically backward village areas to cities and urban townships seeking for works. This eventually lands up many children and young people as easy targets for human trafficking in different forms involving criminals and even unexpected channels such as relatives, friends, people known to them and even their parents.

In *chapter three*, Rosanna Lyngdoh brings in her experiences of using the Impulse Model used in the Impulse Case Info Centre Software Tools based in Shillong, Meghalaya, India to counter human trafficking. She provides several different cases of trafficked victims and the whole network systems in the North East and the mainland India which emerged and developed over the years and helped rescue, rehabilitate and repatriate the survivors by networking with related agencies availing state resources and other options to help the survivors and to counter human trafficking in the region. In *chapter four*, she also discusses the reality of human trafficking in India with a particular focus on North East India specifically that touches on the problems faced by women and children of all sexes.

Then, *chapter five* by Tongpang L. Jamir, deals with legal provisions and enforcement to combat human trafficking. He cogently states that the menace of human trafficking is one of the largest organized crimes across the world that goes hand and glove with drug and arms trafficking. His paper debunks many myths on human trafficking and affirms the reality and truth about the crime and its dynamic operations. He gives lots of information relating to national and international protocols that deal with the crime as well as central and state schemes to address the problems at hand and furnishes some very relevant helpful way forward for concerted efforts by individuals, NGOs and state agents.

In *chapter six*, A. Tali Ao deals with the root causes of human trafficking from the biblical point of view. He notes a complex and complicated domestic violence in the form of partiality and favouritism as the root cause of human trafficking in the story of Joseph. He suggests the victim's acceptance of the perpetrators and forgiveness as a response to the crimes committed by his brothers. At the same time, various biblical injunctions that prohibit human trafficking are dealt with. The biblical response to the evils related to human trafficking is accentuated with the two most important figures in the NT, namely, Jesus and Paul.

Chapter seven is a theological reflection on the menace of human trafficking from a tribal Christian perspective by Lovely Awomi. Her main objective is to provoke the readers for a critical theological discourse on the subject at hand rather than presuming to give any absolute or universal theological response.

Then in *chapter eight*, Johan Mohan Razu argues that the practice of human trafficking existed since the time immemorial even though the modes of operation have undergone changes. According to him, the driving force behind human trafficking is global capitalism through exploitation to gain maximum profit in which women and children are the most targeted group who are treated as market commodities.

Finally, in *chapter nine,* Arenla Longkumer who looks at the problems of human trafficking from a pastoral care perspective describes the trafficked victims' ordeals as traumatic event and experience resulting with multiple physical, psychological and social ailments with lifelong consequences similar to that of post traumatic stress disorder (PTSD). She then advances several ways and means to help trafficked victims to be restored, healed, nurtured, and empowered once again to live a healthy life within the given communities' space and time.

To Wrap Up

The articles were written representing different disciplines such as legal, gender, NGOs, tribals, biblical, theological, ethical, and pastoral/ministerial perspectives. The complex and intricate nature of the criminal activities that impact so devastatingly the total individual, family and community health and life requires such allied and interdisciplinary approach to the problem. However, the papers and the seminar conducted in no way pretend and intend to provide readymade solution to the problem of human trafficking. They only appeal to every right thinking citizen and responsible persons of our communities to be more sensitive, sensible and perceptive about the reality, time and situations of our life. The evils and problems related with human trafficking cannot be dealt with and handled in single handed manner. However, we may see a silver lining in the concerted efforts of responsible individuals and various agencies who keep vigilant and are willing to work together against all odds. This is how we may be able to prevent and combat the menace and rescue at least a few victims, rehabilitate, restore and bring a finite peace and justice to the society and foretaste the infinite and perfect peace here on earth.

Sangtemkala

Keynote Address

Human Trafficking
A Biblical Reflection on Joseph's Story

Asha Sanchu

Human trafficking is defined as the illegal movement of people for the purpose of forced labour or commercial sexual exploitation. According to UN, "Trafficking in Persons as the recruitment, transportation, transfer, harbouring or receipt of persons, by means of the threat or use of force or other forms of coercion, of abduction, of fraud, of deception, of the abuse of power or of a position of vulnerability or of the giving or receiving of payments or benefits to achieve the consent of a person having control over another person, for the purpose of exploitation." It is also termed as "modern day slavery." There are several national and international laws that relate, prevent, prohibit and protect human trafficking and prosecute the traffickers.

Being Christian we often wonder if Bible talks anything on 'Human Trafficking'. Referring to Exodus 21:1-11 many have argued that, Bible encourages slavery. It requires a sociological interpretation in understanding the context and economical vulnerability of those who sold themselves to be slaves to other well to do Hebrews and not to the foreigners and their later freedom or social identity especially in the case of women (21:7-11). However, in the biblical times both polygamy and slavery did exist for their own reasons and were confined within the Hebraic community which is not to be compared with human trafficking.

The Story of Joseph

The story of Joseph could be the story of the first trafficked man in the Bible and the world's first known account of human trafficking. His half-brothers out of jealousy, hatred and finally for self gain trapped him, used force, defrauded and sold him to be a slave to the Egyptians. Looking into the modern day understanding of human trafficking, most of the elements can be found in the trafficking of Joseph, who was sold to be a slave.

The story of Joseph is found in Genesis Ch. 37 – 50. Joseph was the most favoured son of his father Jacob. He was the first born to Jacob's most loving wife Rachel for whom Jacob served as a servant in his father in-law's house for fourteen years (Gen. Ch. 29). Secondly, Joseph was born in Jacob's old age too (Gen. 37:3). Apart from him being loved much by his father, there are other reasons in the Scriptures as to why his half brothers developed hatred and jealousy against Joseph (Genesis 37:2-11). (1) While looking after the flock along with his brothers Joseph would report bad things about his brothers to his father; (2) Due to Jacob's partiality. For instance, giving a beautiful robe to Joseph; (3) Because of the two dreams which he interpreted as his brothers and his parents would bow before him. With all these incidents while his brothers were harboring hatred and jealousy against Joseph in their hearts, Jacob too noted it. However, he let Joseph go in search of his brothers because they had not come back home from pasturing flocks at Shechem. Joseph couldn't find them there and hearing about them went to Dothan where he found them.

Joseph's Trafficking account begins here (Gen. 37:18 - 36) as his brothers expressed their hatred and jealousy in a form of a serious crime that had series of other crimes involved in it; which refers to the modern interpretation of human trafficking:

1. First of all when his brothers saw Joseph forwarding towards them, they recognized from a distance and plotted against him. They planned to kill him by throwing him into a pit. The traffickers are normally more than one. They are never alone. Because this kind of crime requires more than one person to plot and conspire to succeed in their plans.

Therefore, they join with each other or develop a network. Joseph's brothers did the same thing. The moment they saw him they plotted against him or they might have even developed a plan in advance and therefore they moved their location from Shechme to Dothan. The crime connected with human trafficking issues involved here is "criminal conspiracy."

2. As Joseph went closer to his brothers they pulled his robe and threw him into the pit. At first they might have used power and force to get control over him, they might have shouted at him, mocked at him and ridiculed him and then threw him in the pit. It was Reuben's idea not to kill him, but to throw him in the pit so that he may rescue him later. Joseph must have cried aloud for help and his brothers who were close by seemed to have been preparing for their meals. The criminal offences involved here were 'threat', 'force', 'abduction' (kidnapping), 'coercion' or 'intimidation' and 'abuse of power' as they were his elder brothers.
3. Joseph might have been happy to see his brothers as his search ended at Dothan but when he met them he saw their real colors. Joseph must have felt that he had been cheated or he had been deceived. He was defrauded by his brothers. Joseph must have felt terrible after he had fallen in the well. His brothers were about to take their meal without feeling guilty. When Joseph had realized that it was his brothers who had trapped him, his pain might have increased more. Often the victims do not understand the intentions of the traffickers. The first attempt of the traffickers is to defraud by means of false assurance or even by using some kind of trap. The criminal offenses involved here is 'fraud' or 'deception'.
4. The later part of the story was even worse when his brothers saw the Ishmaelite traders. It was Judah, who came up with the idea not to kill him, so that the curse would not come upon the brothers, but to sell him to the traders in exchange of twenty pieces of silver. Joseph was then turned into a commodity for anyone from a human being or a son or a

brother. Criminal offenses directly resulting to recruiting for transferring, transportation, buying or selling, receiving payments for benefit became serious issues of human trafficking as defined in the modern terms.

5. It was still again worse when Joseph became a slave under the ownership of the Ishmaelite traders who sold him further to Potiphar, an officer of Pharaoh the ruler of Egypt. Many scholars refer that until the period of the New kingdom (1550-1175 BCE) Egyptians did not have slavery. The struggle of Joseph continues as he was first put in the house of Potiphar as a slave and then rising to be the CEO in Potiphar's entire business. Then Potiphar's wife Zuleika putting constant pressure on him for sexual seducement and his denial finally ending up with his own imprisonment. Joseph as a trafficked victim was not just a slave, but was also pressurized for sex which is another serious area for the victims of human trafficking.

Looking at Joseph's life we find all the prevailing issues related to the modern understanding of human trafficking. Look at what might have been some of the personal experiences of Joseph after he was trafficked and see how they fit into our understanding of human trafficking? We can well imagine both the physical and emotional experiences Joseph might have gone through. He was a village boy, pampered and much loved by his parents and lived in a closed community where he didn't have enough knowledge of the world outside. He was trafficked, sold and taken as forced labour to a most modern and well developed city of Memphis, as it was the old capital of Egypt. It is like the innocent villagers in our modern society who are trafficked with assurance of jobs in a metro, handsome salary, good place to stay and to make life better and so on. However, finally ending up in deception, hard labour, unhealthy place to stay and sometimes may be in bonded labour. The physical and emotional experience of Joseph might have been similar with many of our time.

It might be accepted by all that Joseph became instrumental in the history of the Israelites' first liberation from the Egyptian bondage and also a model for God's redemption of mankind, but the fact remains that Joseph was a victim of human trafficking. Often it is taken for granted that it was the eternal plan of God to take the Israelites into slavery of the Egyptians and therefore Joseph became an instrument of this. And maybe similarly, when we encounter modern day human trafficking we are often passive about other fellow human beings considering it as their foolishness or fate. The Bible clearly teaches us about the issues related to human trafficking.

What should be our response towards this kind of experience? Should we say, well it is the fate of people that everyone will have to experience like the brothers of Joseph as well as the history? The Bible doesn't directly refer to human trafficking, but it does respond to the issues involved with human trafficking. It does respond to the evils that were involved with what had happened to Joseph.

1. First of all conspiracy is condemned by God (Psalm 83:3).
2. The Mosaic Law condemns defrauding (Leviticus 19:13).
3. The Mosaic Law also condemns kidnapping with death penalty in particular to those who sell people as slaves (Exodus 21:16).
4. The Word of God condemns oppression by using power and force (Zachariah 7:10)
5. The Mosaic Law deals with the freedom of slaves (Exodus 21:1-6). There may be people who sold themselves to be slaves out of their compelling situation. But, the law allows them to be free after six years of service. This had not only created a social security, but also aimed to help the poor to come out of their poverty.
6. The same Mosaic Laws dealing with girls even provided better security that they may not be looked down by others and at the same time their masters were asked to keep them in their house for additional years with proper wages or even to marry them and give respect as equals to their wives. This might have been from a social acceptance point of view.

7. Paul has not only mentioned that there are neither slaves nor free (Galatians 3:28), and also advised Philemon addressing him as his co-worker to accept his runaway slave Onesimus as his brother in Christ (Philemon 1:13).

The Bible speaks much of righteousness and justice. It talks against all kinds of issues involved with modern understanding of human trafficking. Joseph must have felt helpless in his situation. He did not know where his help would come from. Who would help him in the deserted field? And who would take him out of the well? There might have been a great feeling of uncertainty and fear as his situation changed from bad to worse. Word of God says, "Because God was with him (Genesis 39:2) Joseph could rise to great position and power." God fulfilled the dreams of Joseph as he had seen as a child. Joseph was the anointed one through whom God had blessed them as a nation. Not only that, God has avenged and repaid all the evils to his brothers that were done to Joseph.

I would like to leave you with a personal challenge as you take up the cause for the fight for their freedom and justice. Remember that God will be with you, because he takes the side of the oppressed, humble, deceived, poor, orphan and helpless. By doing so you are fighting for God's cause and therefore God will be with you.

1

Women as Victims of Trafficking

"Our lives begin to end the day we become
silent about things that matter"
– Martin Luther King Jr.

Asha Sanchu

Human Trafficking: General Overview

Human Trafficking also known as "modern slavery" a crime against humanity has lately gotten so much attention. Today Human Trafficking is considered a glamorous topic of discussion, debate, social concern/action and challenge. But, the reality of Human Trafficking is not so glamorous. It is ugly and dark. So, much has been talked about on the said subject but very little that has been done especially among the Naga Churches. Human Trafficking is a complex phenomenon that is often driven/ influenced by social, economic, cultural and other factors. Human Trafficking is also a global issue and so demands global attention and action.

Human Trafficking is a crime against humanity. It is the coerced use of human beings as objects of commerce. It involves an act of recruiting, transporting, transferring, harboring or receiving a person through a use of force, coercion or other means for the purpose of exploiting them. It is a re-emergence of slave labour and extreme forms of social exploitation. Trafficking is one of the grave organized crimes, extending beyond boundaries and jurisdictions. Trafficking is also one of the most despicable crimes that one person can commit against another.

Human Trafficking has become globally epidemic and transnational. Statistics show that annually a profit of $32bn is generated from modern day slavery with an estimate of about 21 million people enslaved in it. Women and children are amongst the worst affected and targeted group of population of human trafficking. The exploitation is highly concentrated in the form of sexual exploitation and domestic/forced labour. India stands fourth as the most dangerous place for women/children in the world of which the North eastern region of India is a part. North East India has also become a hotspot for human trafficking as a place of origin, destination and a transit point sharing many national and international borders which are least monitored or unmanned. Because of its clandestine nature, many of the trafficking cases go unreported. Ignorance, gullibility, and poor economic conditions have been found to be the main reasons why the vulnerable section particularly the children and young women are easily enticed. There have been cases of children and youths being trafficked to different states lured with prospect of better education, lucrative jobs and other opportunities, but end up in commercial sexual exploitation, or working in various factories and mines under deplorable conditions, or in other vulnerable conditions. There are several cases of inter-district and interstate human trafficking.

Though Nagaland is a small state in India, it is not immune to the social issue of human trafficking. It has also become a destination, transit point for Human Trafficking. Women/girls are lured with the lucrative promise of better education and job opportunities and are exploited. Statistics shows that children/girls are the most targeted victims of Human Trafficking. Despite the fact that Nagaland is considered as a casteless society and one of safest places for women in India, however, one cannot overlook the fact that gender inequality exist in the society. In Naga context, girls/women become an easy prey for trafficking due to the internal factors of political unrest, economic instability, lack of industries and employment opportunities. As such the traffickers use the tactics of offering better education and livelihood opportunities for luring people.

It is stated that out of the total number of victims trafficked globally, India accounts for half of the world's 30 million slaves. India is the poisonous hub for Trafficking both for Asia and to the world. India is a source, transit and destination country for men, women and children trafficked for the purpose of both forced labour and commercial sexual exploitation. India is also a destination for many girls/women from Nepal and Bangladesh. Though the issue of Human Trafficking is on the rise and has been the most talked subject globally in both secular and religious world. The irony is that it still remains the most neglected issue; outside of the discussion and for the Church.

Women as Victims of Trafficking

Today the face of migration is women, the face of poverty is women, the face of human trafficking is also women and interestingly, the face of the growing church is also women. International Labour Organization (ILO) reports that in forced sexual exploitation and in domestic work, the vast majority of victims are women and girls. Sufficient empirical research information states that structural inequities; including poverty, gender based violence, racism, class and caste-based discrimination and other forms of oppression and marginalization place girls/women at substantially greater risk. Human Trafficking differs from but overlaps with a number of other issues: servile and forced marriage, illicit adoption, domestic violence, sexual abuse and forced labour.

Why are Women the Favoured Target?

Women/girls are typically trafficked into the commercial sex industry for prostitution and other forms of physical and sexual exploitation. Women are also more prone to vulnerability. Sex trafficking generates $27 billion annually and there is always demand. Therefore, demand creates market and market creates supply. Sex tourism, a billion dollar industry also makes women more vulnerable to trafficking. Social inequality, gender preference, social instability and forced marriages where female ratio is skewed compared to men due to infanticide all contributes to women becoming favoured targets for trafficking.

Sex Trafficking

- Sex trafficking generates $27 billion annually
- Sex trafficking is 90% girls and women
- Two million girls and women are forced into prostitution every day. Half of them live in Asia.
- Over 20 million girls/women believed to be working as sexual slaves all over.

Sad Truth

- The favoured target of Human Trafficking is children/girls and women. They make 76% of trafficking.
- Every minute a child goes missing, but only 30% of the total cases are reported.
- 600,000-800,000 people are trafficked across International borders
- It is happening close to home
- Many of the biggest trafficking consumers are developed nations and men from all sectors of society support the trafficking industry.
- There is no profile that encapsulates the "typical" client. It includes both rich and poor.
- Poor families are at higher risk.
- So many laws related to sexual violence and sex trafficking have been amended but there is still a huge gap between enactment and enforcement of these acts.
- Central Asia is a growing region of origin for Human Trafficking (International Organization for Migration). No specific data are given but it is estimated that over 10,000 women are trafficked every year.
- Human Trafficking in Southeast Asia is an "economic whirlwind of substantial force" caused partly by juxtaposition

of extreme poverty with new opportunities for economic exploitation opened by globalization.

- At the end of the day, big fish are hardly caught

Conclusion: In the business of human trafficking, the underlying truth is not sex. It's about money. It's just that sex and free labour sells fats and easy without much effort.

"Let it not be said that I was silent when they needed me"

–William Wilberforce

Few Suggested Readings

- ***Stopping the Traffick: A Christian Response to Sexual Exploitation and Trafficking*: By Glenn Miles and Christa Crawford**
- ***Finding Way Through the Traffick*: By Glenn Miles and Christa C Foster Crawford**
- ***Not for Sale*: By David Batstone**
- ***Sex Trafficking*: *Inside the Business of Modern Slavery*: Siddarth Kara**
- ***Human Trafficking*: *A global Perspective*: By Louise Shelly**
- ***The Natashas*: *Inside the New Global Sex Trade*: By Victor Malarek**
- ***Girls Like Us*: By Rachel Lloyd**
- ***Be the Change*: Zach Hunter**
- ***Caged No More*: By Molly Venzke**
- ***A Crime so Monstrous*: E. Benjamin Skinner**
- ***Deliver Me from Evil*: Kathy Macias**
- ***Collaborating Against Human Trafficking*: By Kristen Foot**
- ***Human Trafficking: A reference Handbook* (Contemporary World Issues): By Alexis A. Aronowitz**
- ***Other Dreams of Freedom*: *Religion, Sex and Human Trafficking*: By Yvonne C. Zimmerram**
- ***Traffick*: Ellen Hopkins**

2

The Prevalence of Trafficking in Child Labour with Special Reference to Our North East Context

T. Chubayanger

The trafficking of human beings is unacceptable under any circumstances, but the trafficking of vulnerable children and young people is a violation of their rights to protection from exploitation, to play, to an education and to health, and to family life. The trafficking of children is not new; it has existed for many years and continues to grow across all continents and all cultures.

Child trafficking is emerging as a global issue; nearly all countries are affected by this criminal violation of children's rights. For some countries, the trafficking of children occurs within national boundaries and remains an essentially national issue. For many, it crosses borders and regions. The victims, mostly separated from their families and communities, end up in prostitution and other exploitative forms of work, such as agriculture, mining, manufacturing, fishing, begging and domestic service. They are vulnerable to abuse and exploitation and are traumatized by this accumulation of denied rights.

International Conventions

The **United Nations Convention on the Rights of the Child** (UNCRC) is a legally-binding international agreement setting out the civil, political, economic, social and cultural **rights** of every **child**, regardless of their race, religion or abilities. The

UNCRC defines the child as a person under 18 years of age. It acknowledges the primary role of parents and the family in the care and protection of children, as well as the obligation of the State to help them carry out these duties. India ratified the UNCRC in the Parliament on 11th December, 1992.

The **ILO Convention on minimum age (138)** is a Convention concerning Minimum Age for Admission to Employment, a Convention adopted in 1973 by the International Labour Organization. It requires ratifying states to pursue a national policy designed to ensure the effective abolition of child labour and to raise progressively the minimum age for admission to employment or work. Article 3 (1) of the Convention prescribes the minimum age for admission to any type of employment or work which by its nature or the circumstances in which it is carried out is likely to jeopardise the health, safety or morals of young person's shall not be less than 18 years.

The **ILO Convention on the Worst Forms of Child Labour (182)** adopted in 1999 identifies the trafficking of children as a practice similar to slavery. The Convention calls for countries to take immediate action to secure the prohibition and elimination of all worst forms of child labour. The Conventions predefined worst forms of child labour are all forms of *slavery* or practices similar to slavery, such as the sale of a child; *trafficking of children*, meaning the recruitment of children to do work far away from home and from the care of their families, in circumstances within which they are exploited; *debt, bondage* or any other form of *bonded labour* or *serfdom*; *forced* or compulsory labour, including forced or compulsory recruitment of *children for use in armed conflict*; Commercial sexual exploitation of children (CSEC), including the use, procuring or offering of a child for *prostitution*, or the production of *pornography* or for pornographic performances; use, procuring or offering of a child by others for illegal activities, also known as *children used by adults in the commission of crime* (CUBAC), including the trafficking or production of drugs; work by its nature that is likely to harm the health, safety or morals of children.

Constitutional Provisions

The Constitution of India places a primary responsibility on the State to ensure that all needs of Children are met and their human rights are fully protected. The specific provisions under the Constitution relating to protection of children from economic exploitation and their education are enshrined in the following Articles below:

Article 21: A Right to Education;
Article 23: Prohibition of traffic in human beings and forced labour;
Article 24: Prohibition of employment of children in factories, etc;
Article 39: The State shall, in particular, direct its policy towards securing that the health and strength of workers, men and women, and the ***tender age of children are not abused*** and that citizens are not forced by economic necessity to enter vocations unsuited to their age or strength.

National Legal Framework

13th June 2017 was a historic moment for India as it took another giant step to affirm her commitment for a child labour free India by ratifying the two Core Conventions of International Labour Organization (ILO) Conventions 138 and Convention 182. Another landmark step in the endeavour to have a child labour free society was the enactment of the amended ***Child and Adolescent labour (Prohibition and Regulation) Act, 1986*** on August 2016, that provides for complete prohibition on employment of children below 14 years in all occupations and processes and prohibits employment of adolescents (14-18 years) in hazardous occupations and processes. The age of admission to employment has been linked to the age of compulsory education under Right to Education Act (RTE), 2009.

Indian Penal Code, 1860: Prohibits kidnapping of a minor for purpose of begging, abduction to subject a person to slavery, buying or disposing off any persons as a slave, habitual dealing in slaves and unlawful compulsory labour.

The Juvenile Justice (Care and Protection of Children) Act, 2015: Prohibition for ostensibly engaging a child and keeping such child in bondage for the purpose of employment or withholding the child's earnings or uses such earnings for one's own purpose (Section 79).

The Bonded Labour System (Abolition) Act, 1976: Prohibits employment of bonded labour and advancement of bonded debt, extracting bonded labour under the bonded labour system.

The Schedule Castes and the Schedule Tribes (Prevention of Atrocities) Act, 1989, prohibits compelling or enticing a member of SC or ST to do 'beggar' or similar form of forced labour or bonded labour other than any compulsory service for public purposes imposed by Government.

India also has legal provisions to counter trafficking as per the **Immoral Trafficking Prevention Act, 1986,** which deals with trafficking of girls and women for prostitution.

Issues and Situations

Having put all the above provisions of law in place, there is still an increasing trend of migration and trafficking of children for labour in different parts of the country. Compelled by the socio-economic conditions, a large number of children are migrating from economically backward areas to cities and urban townships for work. In many of these cases, these children are being directly or indirectly trafficked by middle men, agents, people known to the child, relatives and in some cases even the child's parents themselves who bring them to the employers in the place of destination, who in return extend meagre advances to the parents and give false assurances of lucrative jobs, better life, better education, etc. These children work under highly exploitive situations like very long working hours, no wage or paltry wages where it exists, unhygienic and most difficult working conditions. Such children mostly work in agriculture, Brick Kilns, Stone Quarries, different processes of manufacturing in various home-based industries, construction sites, domestic help, dhabas, tea stalls, apprentice in automobile workshops etc. They are kept of freedom and are vulnerable to abuse and many girls very often fall under the trap of prostitution.

Since India's Northeast shares international borders (which are open and unmanned) with countries like China, Bangladesh, Myanmar, Nepal and Bhutan, it invariably becomes a Source, Transit and a Destination Point. These points provide an easy passage in and out of India for organised human trafficking syndicates to operate undetected. There are instances of trafficking of children for labour from neighbouring countries like Nepal, Bangladesh, and Myanmar etc. So far away from their families, these children are highly vulnerable to all kinds of abuses, including physical and sexual abuse. Issues related to repatriation and rehabilitation of children who are victims of cross border trafficking becomes even more complex and difficult as it involves coordination with other countries from where these children are coming.

North East Prevalence

Magnitude & Incidence of Child Labour in the North-East States (Census 2011) Child Population, Workers & Non-Workers (5-14 yrs)

States	Population	Main workers	Marginal workers	Total Workers	Non-workers
Assam	70,36,066	99,512	1,85,300	2,84,812	67,51,254
Manipur	**6,05,006**	**11,805** (1.95%)	**22,281** (3.68%)	**34,086** (5.63%)	**5,70,920** (94.37%)
Meghalaya	**7,71,788**	**18,839** (2.4%)	**25,630** (3.3%)	**44,469** (5.76%)	**7,27,319** (94.24%)
Mizoram	2,34,769	2793	4985	7778	2,26,991
Nagaland	**4,81,770**	**11,062** (2.3%)	**52,728** (10.9%)	**63,790** (13.2%)	**4,17,980** (86.8%)
Tripura	6,95,425	4998	8562	13,560	6,81,865
Sikkim	1,23,601	2704	7686	10,390	1,13,211

According to **Caritas India** "*Child Right Violation and Trafficking haunting North-East India*" published in September

2017, a report released by National Crime Records Bureau (NCRB) 2015, says that Assam has emerged as the trafficking hub of the country, with 1494 cases, the State accounts for 22% of the total reported cases of trafficking across India. This shows rampant growth in child abuse and Child Rights violation cases in Northeast India. The state also has the highest number of child trafficking (1317) cases, which account for 38% of the national figure. However, this data can be regarded as only the tip of the iceberg. According to a report from Assam's Crime Investigation Department, released during a seminar in October, at least 4,754 children in Assam have gone missing since 2012, of which 2,735 are girls. Child labour and sexual exploitation are the major factor for Child trafficking. The report said that in the past year alone, at least 129 girls were forced into prostitution by traffickers.

Caritas India, during the recent flood carried out assessment and post disaster monitoring wherein found that flood has caused distressed migration of family members for livelihood and children are being lured by trafficking agents. The closure of sick tea garden is another reason making the region fertile for child labour and trafficking.

Sangeeta Tete, the coordinator for women's programs at **PAJHRA**, an NGO in Assam working with Adivasis – (a term commonly used for tribes that migrated from central India to the northeast) says "There have been cases where dead bodies of girls wrapped in bamboo mats were left outside their parents' homes by the traffickers". Traffickers buy young girls for a few thousand rupees, promising parents they will educate the children. Sometimes it's only dead bodies that return home. Adivasis are among the poorest people in Assam, with high levels of illiteracy. Their numbers in the state are estimated to be at least 6 million. "People from Arunachal Pradesh often come to Assam in search of cheap labour, and for a few thousand rupees Adivasis give away their children as young as five years old," Tete says. Once the children are gone, they seldom return.

Prisha (not her real name) a 16 year old Adivasi girl from Okrabasti, a village in northern Lakhimpur was rescued from

Sangram in Arunachal Pradesh after 11 years says "They made me work at home and in the fields during the day. At night, I was made to sleep with different men, including the [trafficker's] family members," she wasn't paid and was given little food. Stories like Prisha's are not new to Assam, which in 2015 reported 1,494 cases of human trafficking, the highest among all 29 Indian states, according to the most recent data from India's National Crime Records Bureau.

The Nobel Peace Prize 2014 laureate and well known Child Rights activist ***Kailash Satyarthi*** expressed concern that Assam and other north-eastern states of India are quickly becoming the hub of child trafficking to places like Delhi, Tamil Nadu, Mumbai and other metros. Satyarthi pointed out Lakhimpur and Kokrajhar districts along with the tea gardens of Udalguri, Sonitpur, Bongaigaon and other backward areas of lower Assam has hot spots for well-organised child traffic rackets.

Founder of Bachpan Bachao Andolan (BBA) and president of Global March Against Child Labour, *Kailash Satyarthi* states that such trafficking takes place under the pretence of providing work as domestic help. Local people are hired to act as agents who then sell these children to placement agencies in Metropolitan cities where they are paid little to nothing. On conducting a raid at a garment factory in Tamil Nadu, the BBA found that more than half the child labourers belonged to the Northeast particularly Assam. "They were all trafficked and bonded. 76 such malnourished children who belonged to Assam and Manipur were also rescued in the previous year. BBA rescue and repatriated 16 adolescent Assamese girls who were trapped into bondage in various places in Delhi. They were trafficked through the local agents operating from Shakurpur, Delhi. The most shameful part of the story was that one of these girls was hesitant to go back home because she was pregnant due to repeated rape," (*Child Trafficking & North East India – Eastern Panorama, Nov. 2014)*.

According to a recent survey by the Assam's Crime Investigation Department, since 2012, the children missing in Assam have been at least 4,754, and 2,753 of them are girls.

Child labour and sexual exploitation are the main factors for child trafficking. The study highlighted that only in the last year; at least 129 girls were forced to prostitute themselves by traffickers. The Northeast Frontier Railway Chief Public Relations Officer Pranav Jyoti Sharma in a release said, "Forty-four children were rescued from trains in Assam last month (Sept. 2017) while being trafficking to other regions." These children were later handed over to their parents and local NGOs. It is to be noted that as per police data, presently, approximately 50,000 trafficked young girls from Assam languish in various households in Arunachal Pradesh who have been engaged as domestic help.

A whopping 250 per cent jump has been witnessed in human trafficking cases in North Eastern States this year as compared to 2015, with most being reported from Assam. Of the total 1,539 human trafficking cases registered in 2015, as many as 1,494 were from Assam, 20 from Meghalaya, 16 from Tripura, 6 from Nagaland and 3 from Arunachal Pradesh. The reported cases are mostly children trafficked for different purposes. The total number of such cases reported in these eight states in 2014 was 435, while just 186 in 2013 *(The Indian Express, December 2016)*.

Hasina Kharbhih *(Kharbhi October 2017)* founder of **Impulse NGO Network** (INGON) and recipient of the *CNN-IBN* India Positive Award, puts on record that India's Northeast shares international borders with countries like China, Bangladesh, Burma, Nepal and Bhutan; it invariably becomes an easy passage for organised human trafficking. From the rat-hole miners of Jaintia Hills to the flesh trade in Silchar. INGON discovered that a massive percentage of the rural children in the villages of Meghalaya had gone missing. Deeper research revealed that due to lack of income sources, the villagers would send their children to do odd jobs like serving tea at tea stalls or run similar errands at token shops. Traffickers were taking this opportunity to lure these with promises of well-paid jobs and cross them over to other states, districts or countries with considerable ease.

Until the National Green Tribunal (NGT), effected a directive passed on April 17, 2014, banning rat-hole mining in the state of Meghalaya, there were acute demand for young children for coal mining in Meghalaya's Jaintia Hills that engages slave child labour who were trafficked from Nepal and Bangladesh for low wages. Approximately 70,000 children, from Bangladesh, Nepal and Meghalaya's villages were engaged in this dangerous enterprise. The reason why little children are employed in this business is technical as the mining here requires manual recovery of coal from the deepest recesses of the earth via tunnel-like passages. These are so narrow that it is traversable only by little children. Children as young as five were working in these mines. Children have been dying in these rat holes and the dead bodies are not being taken back because it's not possible to get them out. They are not even being reported because, in the context of Meghalaya, they are illegal migrants. Now that the illegal mining is banned, the disturbing question remains, ***where have these mining children gone?***

There is huge demand for young girls from the Northeast for job opportunities within India and Southeast Asia. Lured by unauthorised recruiting agencies, these girls are either coerced into the commercial sex trade or domestic work. Last year, INGON rescued six girls from Mizoram, who were being taken to a neighbouring country. The destination points are usually Singapore and Malaysia. Recently, eight Manipuri girls, who were being trafficked to Singapore by members of an international gang, were rescued in Myanmar.

While young girls are trafficked for an offshore market, they do have a huge demand in the domestic flesh trade business too. A very audacious example is the organised red-light area in the heart of Silchar town, the headquarters of Cachar district, Assam. According to Immoral Trafficking Prevention Act (ITPA), 1956, a prostitution centre cannot exist in a public place, but Silchar is an exception. Fresh girls are brought from different states and sold in the brothel on a frequent basis. Another worrying factor is the demand for brides in the states of Haryana, Uttar Pradesh and Rajasthan, which have a poor sex ratio. Young girls are trafficked from Assam often to be forcibly married off to men in those states.

Traffickers often change their victims' names to make it more difficult for families and police to track them down.

(*North East Today, 10th November 2016*) Human trafficking, particularly child trafficking, has been on the rise in Manipur though it largely remained elusive from the public domain. The alarming rate is evident as altogether 58 reported cases of child trafficking have been recorded within first six months of 2016. It is learnt that from 2013 to June 2016, 62 cases of child trafficking were recorded. In the month of February 2016 alone, 29 children of Churchandpur, Ukhrul and Imphal were reportedly rescued from Meghalaya. In April, 17, 2016, children from Sugnu, Thoubal district were intercepted by Sekmai police along the National Highway 102 (Imphal-Dimapur road), who were on their way to Tamil Nadu and in June 12 children from Churachandpur district were reportedly rescued from Tamil Nadu. 21 children were rescued from Tulihal Airport by the Manipur Commission for Protection of Child Rights (MCPCR) and eight children from Kolkata Airport by Child Welfare Committee (CWC) Kolkata in mid July 2016.

Imphal Oct 1, 2017: Eight Manipuri girls, who were being trafficked to Singapore by members of an international gang, were rescued in Myanmar and brought home. Not only women or girls but even boys are being trafficked for sending them as domestic workers in countries such as Singapore and elsewhere. In a recent incident that has come to light, the Anti-Human Trafficking Cell of Imphal west police have intercepted a boy from Tulihal Airport trying to board a flight to Singapore with fake documents. Initial investigation revealed that the boy was to be employed as domestic worker at Singapore and was accompanied by a woman from Senapati who had earlier been involved in a human trafficking case. The incident comes barely a day after eight young boys were intercepted from the Tulihal Airport by the same Anti-Human Trafficking Cell while trying to board flight to Chennai via Kolkata without proper documents. Although, the estimated number of trafficked children in Manipur is 500 in the last 7 years, a large number of children and girls have remained untraceable, hence exact figure of already trafficked children remained unknown.

The first case of child trafficking in Manipur was reported way back in 2005 when three girls from Borayamgbi of Bishnupur district and Hatta Golapati of Imphal East district were rescued from Tulihal Airport along with doctors, who were heading to Chandigarh. Of all the cases till date, the most shocking case emerged in the year 2013 following the rescue of 32 children of Ukhrul district, rescued from 'Grace Church Home' in Jaipur, Rajasthan. The main culprit of the cases Jacob Johns, a pastor in the 'Grace Church Home' reportedly raped 13 girls of the total rescued children.

Human trafficking in Tripura along Indo-Bangla border especially in Dharamnagar is on the rise. Porous International Border along Indo-Bangladesh not only provides safe corridors to traffickers but also acts as easy gates for human trafficking, especially minors. According to Tripura Infoway News *(TIWN June 30 2017)*, trafficking in women and children has dramatically increased in Dharmanagar. In most cases, traffickers are found to have lured their victims to come with them by promising them good jobs, quality education and better housing.

Recently, A total of five children from a village of Gomati District, trafficked to Bangladesh by a couple, were handed over to their family. The Bangladesh police handed over the five children to the Tripura police at Belonia Check Post (South District). All the children are between the ages of 8 to 11 years old and are all residents of Purba Gokulpur under RK Police Station in Gomati District.

Most of the trafficking rackets in Tripura consists of women who comes from outside state and clutches the minor girls from the interior part of the State as children are easier to smuggle through borders, cheaper and easier to control. According to TIWN the trafficking racket has an administrative reach in Tripura by which they manage fake passports and sent the minors outside India. Many minors are sold through this racket in other parts of the country and even outside the country. The highway networks in the region connect many national and international destinations.

The destinations are usually New Delhi, Mumbai, Pune, Goa and Kolkata and extend as far as Thailand and Singapore.

In one incident during March 2015 *(Tripura Business Standard)*, 19 tribal children were rescued from Guwahati railway station in Assam by security forces and Childline, an NGO, and handed over to their parents at Kanchanpur in Tripura according to north *Tripura* district magistrate Sandeep Rajan Rathod. Of the 19 children, all were below 18 years of age, 11 belonged to the Reang refugees of Mizoram who are currently living in seven camps in Tripura.

In the year 2010, 150 children from Arunachal Pradesh have been trafficked to Phuntsok Choeling monastery in Kathmandu with the promise of a better education. Six of the 150 children have been reported missing from the monastery, located in Swayambhu. The children were reported to have gone missing after one of them telephoned their parents in Arunachal, complaining about the cruel treatment meted out to them at the monastery. In an exclusive recorded conversation available with Sunday Mid Day, Wangdi, the alleged child-trafficker admitted, "I have been sending children to Kathmandu since the year 2006. Till date, I have sent 70 children to the monastery. My only duty was to hand them over to the monastery. I was not concerned with their daily activities in the monastery." This report is just one example of many monasteries involved in such activities.

While many cases of child trafficking from Arunachal is reported till the recent past, another flip side is that children mostly girls, are trafficked to neighbouring Arunachal Pradesh from Lakhimpur and Dhemaji district of Assam and are sold to buyers to be engaged in domestic help amounting to the state of slavery. Minor girls from almost all communities, mostly from the poor, landless families of the immigrant Muslim community are trafficked to Arunachal Pradesh from the Bangalmara, Nowboicha, Laluk, Dejoo areas of Lakhimpur district to be used as slaves in various households. Most of such cases remain unreported in the nearest police stations and it comes out only when someone returns home as escapees.

Crisis of a different kind is griping the quake affected areas, trying to grapple with the devastation caused by the 6.9 magnitude quake that had hit on September 18, 2011. The survivors of the quake mainly from remote areas who have lost their families and support system, have become vulnerable to human trafficking. Studies conducted by numerous worldwide and Indian agencies clearly indicate that women and children are highly vulnerable to trafficking in such conditions.

According to Asian Age, a joint team of Delhi and Sikkim police rescued a 16-year-old from a brothel in G.B. Road, New Delhi on August 2016. A police official said that it was first of its kind case when a trafficked minor girl from Sikkim is rescued from the capital. A senior police official has informed that after Assam, which sees one of the highest numbers of cases as far as the trafficking of minor girls is concerned, and several other north-eastern states, Sikkim could be the latest where trafficking rackets linked to Delhi are spreading their tentacles.

Mizoram is the first state in the northeast to formulate a ***'Victims of Crime Compensation Scheme'***, the United Nations Office on Drugs and Crime (UNODC) report said. It added that the scheme was formulated in 2011 to ensure that the victims of human trafficking were rehabilitated. The burden of financial assistance for the victims of human trafficking is shared by the Centre and the state government.

According to a recent report by the Anti-trafficking unit in Mizoram, since Myanmar's democratic government took over in 2016, it has been easier to travel through the country and traffickers have stepped up activity. "The Myanmar route to South East Asia is seeing increasing trafficking because for many miles on both sides of the border, the people are the same-speaking the same language, looking the same," said Thianghlima Pachuau, head of the Mizoram police force, "We have had tragic cases in the region. In one instance a girl died in Singapore but could not be brought home (to India) since her documents indicated she was a Myanmar national. Her parents never got closure. The girls don't realise that when they travel on the fake passport of another country, there is very little we can do to help them when they are abused or in trouble. Getting a passport and travel documents in Myanmar is easy for the agents," he said.

On 21 March, 2017, Dr. Temsula Ao, Chairperson of Nagaland State Commission for Women (NSCW) informed that in 2016 there was not a single record of human trafficking in Nagaland as per Nagaland Police source. She believed people did not lodge complaints due to many societal compulsions. Dr. Temsula stressed that hiding incidents of human trafficking for fear of social stigma or retaliation only enlarges the perpetrators' trade and earning and put more people into miserable broken lives.

The Police data indicates that in Nagaland a person goes missing every fourth day where 83 percent are below the age of 18 and 13 percent have been reportedly trafficked, and 35 percent are untraced. A total of 51 children from different Northeast states including 8 children from Nagaland rescued from two illegal children homes run by a pastor in Jaipur. The main accused in the trafficking of children from Nagaland, Pastor Jacob John, son of K. K. John has been brought to Nagaland from Jaipur by Jalukie police. The rescued children came from remote villages in Peren District. Their parents were convinced with free education in a city along with free lodging and food.

The SCPS Nagaland has been actively involved in Anti-Trafficking campaign in Nagaland. SCPS was instrumental in rescuing 6 trafficked children from Kolkata on 13th April 2012 and 6 trafficked children of Nagaland were rescued from Coimbator in the year 2013. There were 8 children among the 51 children rescued from two illegal children home in Jaipur and on 4th April 2014, SCPS brought back the 8 children from Jaipur, Rajasthan.

According to Neimenuo Kengurusie in *Human Trafficking in North East India: Patterns and Emerging Trends, Journal of North East India Studies-30th July 2017* says, the issue of human trafficking in Naga society appears to be low-key on the surface but a closer look reveals that the menace of human trafficking is taking root. The rise in cases on human trafficking in recent times is an alarming trend that needs immediate attention.

Case Study: Dr. Henry proclaimed himself to be the Director of the 'Truth Light Healing Ministry' of Assam, Manipur and Nagaland, a ministry that claims to be affiliated to the American Baptist Convention. It was learnt that in 2009, Dr. Henry and Mrs. Sarah of the same ministry had visited the Samziuram and New Jalukie village under the Peren District and during their visit, they advocated for free education and accommodation for children in the 'Gypsy orphan children home' that is located at Andhra Pradesh. They convinced the parents to avail themselves of this opportunity to send their children for free theological studies under the care and guidance of the Evangelical Association for Revival Education (EARE), which is an NGO based in the Guntur district of Andhra Pradesh. Together, the parents of twenty nine children decided to avail of the opportunity for their children and registered them for the programme. The children were then escorted by Dr. Henry and Sarah to Dimapur and from there, they left for Andhra Pradesh. Later on, it was discovered that the children were not sent to schools as promised but were ill treated and made to perform numerous tasks without proper food and lodging.

According to Neimebuo, Nagaland is not only a source state but also a transit point for trafficked victims from India to other countries. Pangsa under Tuensang district and Dimapur in Nagaland are the transit centres for trafficking. Women and children from Assam, Nagaland and Bangladesh are trafficked through the Pangsa International border, and then moved out to Myanmar and other South East Asian countries through the golden triangle. Dimapur is a transit point for women and children trafficked from Assam especially from upper Assam, Lumding and Guwahati. From Dimapur, they are moved to Moreh in Manipur or international border at Tuensang in Nagaland to the golden triangle (Sen & Nair, 2005). Nagaland has also become a destination point for trafficked victims particularly from Assam, where they are inducted into commercial sex trade and domestic work.

According to a study conducted by a local NGO, Prodigals' Home, every three and half day a person goes missing in Nagaland and that 83 percent of missing reports are of children below 18 years of age. Dimapur district recorded the highest number of missing children at 68 percent (Prodigals' Home, 2009). The study indicates that human trafficking may be one of the main reasons behind those missing children. According to the latest report from Dimapur Police, in 2015 alone, about 115 cases of missing women and children were registered, out of which 67 were traced while 48 remains untraced.

Human trafficking is the third largest organized crime after drugs and the arms trade across the globe and is one of the major problems in India. Northeast being riddled with conflict and poor infrastructure has been the target of many human traffickers. A study across the states of Northeast has shown an increasing number of human trafficking mostly women and girls and over the years, there has been a rise in reports of missing girls from remote region of the eight states, which authorities believe is due to trafficking.

The magnitude of the problem as it exists in India's North Eastern Region is alarming and it continues to grow. While there are a number of laws protecting child rights in India, they are seldom enforced strictly in the North-east States. Lack of proper monitoring system and weak enforcement of other existing laws, is one factor why the region is becoming a safe haven for traffickers especially child traffickers thus most cases are going unnoticed or unreported. This can be justified by the latest data published by Press Information Bureau, Government of India, Ministry of Women and Child Development which indicates a grim statistics on the number of Women and Children Trafficked during last two years.

Total Number of Women and Children Trafficked During the Year 2015 & 2016

Sl. No.	State/UT	2015		2016		
		Women	Children (Below 18 Year)	Women	Children (Below 18 Year)	Data not received for the month
1	Arunachal Pradesh	10	11	3	2	
2	Assam	187	129	163	130	
3	Manipur	0	3	16	9	
4	Meghalaya	1	1	8	1	
5	Mizoram	0	0	2	2	
6	Nagaland	2	2	0	0	Dec.
7	Sikkim	0	0	1	1	
8	Tripura	1	5	5	6	
	Total	201	151	198	151	

Press Information Bureau, Government of India, Ministry of Women and Child Development (09-March-2017)

Besides other underlying factors, the problem of scores of youth and children getting trafficked across the border is society's negligence to acknowledge what's happening. Once we accept that there is rampant human trafficking from and to the Northeast of India, we'll be able to decipher the cause that leads to it.

3

Impulse Model and the Impulse Case Info Centre Software Tools to Counter Human Trafficking

Rosanna Lyngdoh

In the year 1999, when the email campaign to fight human trafficking was initiated by ATSEC (Action against Trafficking and Sexual Exploitation of Children) to all the partners in India, Impulse NGO Network received three cases of trafficked minor girls from Northeast India from an Organisation in Mumbai.

The girls were brought to Shillong under the custody of Impulse NGO Network and were kept in the newly created extension shelter home for trafficked survivors, in the premises of the Observation Home, with the written permission of the then Director of Social Welfare, Government of Meghalaya.

With limited resources, it was an added load to Impulse NGO Network, to repartriate the girls to their homes, one being from the state of Tripura.

Impulse NGO Network sought the help of the State Government of Tripura and its State partner organisation "Voluntary Health Association of Tripura" to help repartriate and reintegrate the girl back to her family in Tripura.

When Human Trafficking was then, not known or heard of in the North East of India, the rescue of the three girls blazed a trail of path to the problem of trafficking in the region. This became quite a significant breakthrough.

Having limited resources, it was difficult for Impulse NGO Network to rescue, rehabilitate and repartriate the survivors of human trafficking. Hence, networking with other agencies and using the state resources was an option to help the survivors and counter human trafficking in the region.

Impulse NGO Network saw the potential and the success in networking with other agencies to curb human trafficking and hence developed the Impulse Model earlier known as Meghalaya Model which took shape and set off as a successful model to address human trafficking in the North East Region as well as other neighbouring countries of the region.

The birth of Impulse Model was the accumulation of many cases of human trafficking that Impulse NGO Network intervened, where the help and network of other organisations, Law Enforcement and State Government Agencies were needed.

Introduction to Impulse Model

Impulse Model (formerly known as Meghalaya Model) is an internationally acknowledged, holistic method to address human trafficking by engaging the necessary public and private sector stakeholders to work in collaboration to strengthen each others' work. Each of the stakeholders (including government departments and law enforcement agencies, civil society organizations and media) has their own mandate under the Impulse Model and is connected to each other through Impulse Case Info Centre. The stakeholders working in close coordination with each other ensures that there will not be overlapping of efforts and resources, making the stakeholders' work become more effective.

The Impulse Model's case management system follows the following elements, called the **6 R's: Reporting, Rescue, Rehabilitation, Repatriation, Re-integration and Re-compensation.** Each of these elements in case management is crucial and must be conducted with efficient, victim-friendly procedures, engaging the necessary stakeholders in the process. Therefore, to provide holistic anti-human trafficking response and effective case management, the tools of the **6 P's are**

necessary: Partnership, Prevention, Protection, Policing, Press and Prosecution.

The Impulse Model was conceptualized by Founder and Chair of Board, Impulse NGO Network, Ms. Hasina Kharbhih, who received the prestigious Ashoka Fellowship for the innovation

The Six Ps of Impulse Model

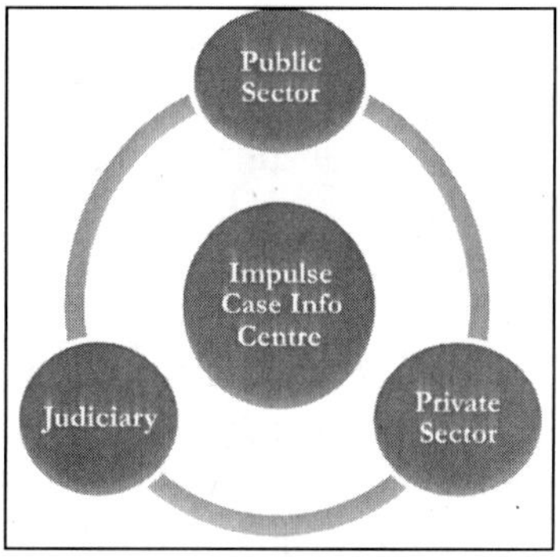

The Six Ps are the tools of Impulse Model, that enable the stakeholders to follow the case management procedure of the 6 Rs. These 6 Ps are Partnership, Prevention, Protection, Policing Press and Prosecution.

Partnership

The Impulse Model provides a National and International platform for the collaboration between public and private sector stakeholders. The combined strength of these partnerships is the most essential element in countering human trafficking.

Impulse Case Info Centre (ICIC) brings the stakeholders periodically together in meetings and conferences, to ensure that all the stakeholders can express themselves with regards to the successes and challenges they face.

Prevention

Awareness Programmes

Awareness programmes and livelihood initiatives are very effective methods to be used in combating human trafficking. Impulse NGO Network conducts awareness programmes for communities directly as well as training both private and public sector agencies on how to incorporate to their on-going programmes an anti-human trafficking component. Awareness on human trafficking can be raised through various methods, starting from films, street plays, pamphlets, posters or postcard, lectures or public service announcements to social media campaigns.

Awareness programmes also function as outreach programmes, as often people recognize that it may have already happened to someone they know and they can report the incident.

Lack of employment possibilities leave people very vulnerable to human trafficking, as many people migrate unsafely to find work. Carefully designed and implemented livelihood initiatives in rural areas give people the possibility to have a sustainable income in their villages, reducing the incentive to migrate.

Livelihood Initiatives

Since the early years of operation, Impulse NGO Network has been implementing various livelihood programmes in the rural communities of North East India to prevent unsafe migration that often leads to human trafficking and explaoitation.

Understanding the need of a sustainable livelihood initiative, a sister concern of Impulse NGO Network, Impulse Social Enterprises (ISE) was established in 2009. Empower business initiative of ISE mobilizes rural artisans, of which several are survivors of violence, located in various different clusters across North East India.

Empower has an innovative approach to prevent unsafe migration by addressing the needs of the rural communities; empowering the rural artisans to become independent entrepreneurs with professional dignity but at the same time to offer them secure and sustainable income. The initiative gives incentive to rural communities to work and make their own living but also giving them the flexibility of entrepreneurship. Through the revival of traditional artisan products in the rural communities using locally available raw materials livelihood opportunities are enhanced benifitting many. The initiative also protects the traditional patterns and designs of various tribes in the region.

The artisans have control over their time and production, granting them freedom to work when they want, where they want, and as much as they want. Therefore, the initiative caters especially to the needs of the rural women who often have to take care of other family responsibilities. An assured market for their products creates security and sustainability for their families and has a positive impact on the entire community, reducing unsafe migration. This makes people less vulnerable to human trafficking.

Protection

Impulse NGO Network ensures that the survivors of human traffkcing are provided with the necessary support services as per the law by trained and sensitized professionals. All the stakeholders of different professions that come across with human trafficking cases must understand the trauma the victims go through. They must be aware of the victim-friendly procedures and minimum standards to give best possible protection to the victims.

The aspect of protection therefore includes policy making and ensuring that the services as per the law are in place in all the states and districts.

Policing

Impulse NGO Network organizes trainings, consultations and develops handbooks for police in order to sensitize police personnel to good practices in countering the issue of human trafficking.

Impulse Case Info Center collaborates closely with law enforcement agencies, especially with Anti-Human Trafficking Units to ensure that all the human trafficking cases are managed accordingly. All the cases that ICIC receives are referred to Anti-Human Trafficking Units and First Information Reports are always filed at the local police stations. ICIC provides the law enforcement agencies with constant technical support during the different stages of dealing with human trafficking cases.

Handbook for Law Enforcement on Trafficking in Persons 2006
Created by Impulse NGO Network and North Eastern Police Academy Supported by the UNODC

The handbook was created to offer basic training to law enforcement personnel to help them combat human trafficking in their jobs. It aims to create knowledge and understanding among law enforcement, cultivate a victim-friendly attitude, train law enforcement in skills and techniques, and link and create skilled persons from multi-disciplinary professions. Planning for the handbook, a planning workshop was held, and multiple drafts of the handbook were made in 2006 and circulated to various people, organisations, and agencies for editing and revising. It includes input from nodal officers of anti-trafficking in the eight North East states, a core technical team, a technical team, NGOs, lawyers, academia, and the United Nations. It also includes feedback from the Director General of Police from North Eastern States Bureau of Police Research and Development Ministry of Home Affairs (BPRD), Government of India. The final Handbook was published and circulated September 2007.

Press

Media is a powerful tool to raise awareness on human trafficking as well as to locate the missing persons. However, it is crucial that media personnel understand the issue of human trafficking extremely well, to be able to inform people about the issue clearly and correctly. While publishing stories on human trafficking, it is important that media personnel are sensitive towards the victims of human trafficking and their families – the personal details of human trafficking victims should not be published in any case. Media personnel must also understand the trauma the victims have gone through; in case they have a possibility to interview a survivor, they must understand what they can ask and how to ask questions, to avoid further victimization of the victims.

Impulse Case Info Centre trains media personnel to publish articles and report on human trafficking. The trained media personnel become Impulse Case Info Centre Media Partners, with whom partnership and collaboration is established. Impulse Case Info Centre provides the correct information regarding the cases then the media personnel can publish the story according to the guidelines, protecting the identity of the victims.

Best Practice in Action: Media Campaign against Child Labour in Coal Mines

In the coal mines of Jaintia Hills, Meghalaya, thousands of children are working in hazardous conditions. In the area, mining is done unscientifically, using the traditional mining method called Rat Hole Mining, where the labourers are forced to crawl into narrow tunnels deep under the ground to collect the coal, without any safety equipments or structures. Many of the children working in the mines have been trafficked, sold as bonded labour to the mine owners.

Impulse NGO Network conducted a variety of studies in the area, mapping the mines and child workers. The horrifying results were presented to the both State and Central Government. However, no concrete action was taken to help these child labourers.

The Impulse NGO Network team in addition to developing strong participatory research skills has established a small media partner's network of media partners across India and globally through AHRC Urgent Appeal and also the Global Development Network (GDN). The network provides support in transforming the research generated by Impulse NGO Network into media friendly messages, and working jointly on what component each media houses has to highlight, to retain non duplication and have a systematic approach. The team used this platform to take forward the cause of the mine labourers.

Impulse NGO Network, therefore, in the above instance started a strong media campaign, to create mass awareness on the issue. Numerous national and international media (New York Times, Los Angeles Times, France 24, France 2, France 5, SBS One, ABC, CNN-IBN, Hindustan Times, Tehelka etc.) visited Jaintia Hills, featuring stories of the child rights violation in the area all around the globe. It is therefore an important learning of the exercise that it is necessary to generate and use a form of evidence that substantiates the research – the use of photo and video to support data generated in interviews.

The media campaign created strong demands to address the issue of child labour in the coal mines. This has led to change in the attitudes, the issue has been given more attention in the government agenda and a policy level changes.

Impulse NGO Network filed a Public Interest Litigation towards the illegal method of mining in the state. Currently, due to the National Green Tribunal Order, the Rat Hole Mining has been banned and recompensation is being offered to the child workers.

Prosecution

Victims must get justice, which is a crucial step for the victims to become survivors. Failure to prosecute effectively (impunity) encourages human traffickers to continue to flout the laws. A human trafficking case is not successfully closed without the trafficker being convicted as per the law.

The victims and their families must be provided legal support, assistance to file law suits against the offenders as well as counselling through the process. The necessary paperwork and documentation must be in place for the prosecution process. Therefore, the case documentation of Impulse Case Info Centre is critical; all the information related to the case must be available, clear and in order.

Impulse Case Info Centre follows the prosecution to ensure that the process is being followed up properly and swiftly. Impulse Case Info Centre follows up with the police on the progress of the case and contacts higher authorities if there is an unreasonable delay. Impulse Case Info Centre also follows up with lawyer on the progress of the case after the Charge sheet (a formal document of accusation prepared by law enforcement agencies) is filed; and supports the child and family throughout the legal process with counseling.

The prosecution pillar includes the training of the judiciary and lawyers. They are trained and sensitized to understand the particuliarities of the crime of human trafficking.

The Impulse Model (Impulse Case Info Centre) has been selected as top 3 in the world for its Innovative Practice. In the 13th Annual Global Development Conference held at Budapest for Global Development Awards and Medals Competition 2011, Japanese Award for most Innovative Development Project, Impulse Case Info Centre has won the second prize in the competition among top three models in the world in the year 2012.

Impulse Case Info Centre Software

Impulse Case Info Centre (ICIC) is the Heart of the Impulse Model, being responsible that all the human trafficking cases reported to the network of stakeholders are managed appropriately, following the procedure of **6 R's.** Impulse Case Info Centre records, compiles and keeps track of all relevant information on human trafficking cases. Impulse Case Info Centre created a case database system that is continuously shared with the Anti-Human Trafficking Units (AHTUs) set up by Government of India, as well as with other stakeholders, to provide updated information on human trafficking cases and suspected human traffickers. This has resulted in overall increased reliability and efficacy of response to human trafficking and strengthened the anti-human trafficking network through increased and continuous communication.

Hence, Impulse Case Info Centre works towards that all human trafficking victims are traced and rescued. After which, Impulse Case Info Centre focuses on the needs of human trafficking survivor, including legal support network, services such as a victim-protection, post-rescue livelihood/

vocational training, counselling and medical care. For successful management of each of these steps, assistant and support of different stakeholders are required.

Impulse Case Info Centre manages human trafficking cases by following the 6 R's of Impulse Model.

Reporting

Anyone can report a human trafficking case to Impulse Case Info Centre, whether it be a concerned family member or a stakeholder of the Impulse Model. A case can be referred to Impulse Case Info Centre at any stage; from the moment a person goes missing, right through to when a rescue operation has already taken place and the victim is in need of repatriation, re-integration or re-compensation.

The Impulse Case Info Centre Case Manager assists in filing an FIR (First Information Report) at the Police Station, if not already filed.

Once a case has been reported, Impulse Case Info Centre documents the case in the Impulse Case Info Centre database, and immediately refers the case to the respective AHTU (Anti-Human Trafficking Unit) and partner organisations at the source and destination points, both nationally and internationally. Impulse Case Info Centre provides support to the stakeholders in the process of tracing the victim.

Rescue

Rescue operations are carried out by the respective Anti-Human Trafficking Units, along with Impulse Case Info Centre or an Impulse Case Info Centre's State Partner Organisation. Impulse Case Info Centre provides training to the law enforcement agencies and partner organisations on all aspects of their responsibilities during the rescue operations, taking into consideration pre-rescue planning and post-rescue requirements as well as on victim-friendly and gender/child sensitive approach to conduct the rescue.

Rehabilitation

Rehabilitation process starts immediately after the person is rescued. Impulse Case Info Centre collaborates with the Social Welfare Departments of respective states to provide short term shelter for the rescued persons. In case the government shelter is not available, Impulse Case Info Centre refers the rescued persons to an NGO run shelter home that have been notified by the government.

During the short-term rehabilitation, Impulse Case Info Centre ensures that medical and other support services are provided to the rescued persons as per the need. Moreover, during the short-term rehabilitation period, actions are being taken to identify the best long-term integration for the survivor.

Repatriation

Based on Home Investigation Report (HIR) by Impulse Case Info Centre, State Partner Organization, AHTU or qualified social worker, the process of repatriation is initiated. HIR is conducted to identify if it is safe for the survivor to return to their home, ensuring that they wouldn't be returning to a cycle of violence.

Custody of the survivor will be passed via a letter of consent, if it is deemed safe for them to return to their family. If the survivor is not able to return to their family, Impulse Case Info Centre collaborates with the Social Welfare Department to arrange long-term accommodation for them; also offering the survivor training, education or employment, depending on the person's age and personal interests.

In the case of international repatriation, restoration procedure varies depending on the victim's country of origin.

Re-Integration

Impulse Case Info Centre and partner organizations assist the Social Welfare Department to ensure that the survivor has access to education, training or employment. This is essential for the survivor to begin the process of rebuilding his/her life. Impulse Case Info Centre and the partner organizations follow up with the survivors for a period of two years, to ensure that the survivor is safe and that the re-integration programme developed for them is bringing results. This is carried out with a high degree of discretion, so that the survivors have time to heal and do not fall prey to further victimization.

Re-Compensation

Several states of India have introduced re-compensation schemes that include re-compensation for victims of human trafficking. In the case of the fatality of the victim, the family of the victim may also be eligible for re-compensation. Impulse Case Info Centre collaborates with State Legal Services Authorities to ensure that all the survivors of human trafficking are granted financial re-compensation.

Impulse Case Info Centre Software Under Impulse Model of Impulse NGO Network

The idea of creating an AHT Software evolved, when the number of human trafficking cases in the Impulse Case Info Centre Database was becoming hard to manage manually. Impulse Case Info Centre recognized that the Anti-Human Trafficking Units of India crucially needed an AHT Software for systematic documentation of human trafficking cases.

The Impulse Case Info Centre Software provides the Anti-Human Trafficking Units a fast and systematic communication channel across the country to share case information, documents, and updates on the human trafficking cases. All the Anti-Human Trafficking Units have their specific user account in the AHT Software, enabling them to see only the cases that they have registered or cases that have been referred to them. This ensures that necessary confidentiality and privacy standards are followed. However, the Software has an alert-feature, enabling different units to realize if any other unit is, or has been, managing a case involving the same human trafficking victim or the same human trafficker.

Moreover, the Impulse Case Info Centre Software is automatically colliding statistical information on high prevalence source and destinations areas for human trafficking; the trafficking methods and routes, along with general profile of human trafficking victims and traffickers.

The Software has been developed by Speech Ware Net IIT Incubation Guwahati and has been launched for the eight states of North East India, given free-of-charge to the AHTUs. The Software will also be revised to be suitable to be available for Myanmar Anti-Human Trafficking Forces. Therefore, the Software will provide both national and international communication channel for Anti-Human Trafficking Units to share information and collaborate in human trafficking cases.

Background

All the human trafficking cases reported to Impulse Case Info Centre, are recorded to the database using standardized formats. Impulse Case Info Centre ensures the constant update of the case files by contacting the stakeholders of the specific case, enquiring news as well as informing the stakeholders on the progress of the cases.

Through this database system, the Impulse Case Info Centre has become the hub of AHT-related real-time information. This has resulted in overall increased reliability and efficacy of response to human trafficking and has strengthened the anti-human trafficking network through increased and continuous communication.

Thus the Impulse Model, through the Impulse Case Info Centre, acts as a centre of information: a) as a comprehensive database; b) as a referral system linking various stakeholders as per the need of the victim; c) as a capacity-building tool for the stakeholders on maintaining and sharing information, through the Impulse Case Info Centre; and d) improves the collaboration and coordination among the stakeholders.

Objectives of the Impulse Case Info Centre Software

The Impulse Case Info Centre Software provides the needed national and international link for the Anti-Human Trafficking

Units to collaborate in reporting and sharing information on human trafficking cases.

The Impulse Case Info Centre Software Enables

1. Systematic case documentation for cases of human trafficking.
2. Fast and continuous communication among Anti-Human Trafficking Units nationally and internationally.
3. Centralization of required formats and toolkits for Anti-Human Trafficking
4. Centralization of stakeholder's contacts
5. Platform for statistical information on human trafficking trends nationally and internationally
6. Alert system – in case the details of human trafficking victim or suspected trafficker has already been inserted in the Software in another registered case, the Software will send a notification alert

Impulse NGO Network

The Impulse NGO Network is a non-profit human rights organization based out of Shillong, Meghalaya in the Northeast of India. Founded in 1993 by Hasina Kharbhih, Impulse NGO Network is one of the first and foremost organizations to have started work to counter the rampant human trafficking in the region.

Impulse NGO Network's anti-human trafficking work expands across the eight states of Northeast India, Nepal, Bangladesh and Myanmar, where the internationally recognized Impulse Model (Meghalaya Model) has been replicated. Moreover, the organization has several networking partners around the globe, especially in the South and South East Asia.

Website:
www.impulsengonetwork.org
www.impulsesocialenterprises.com

4

Human Trafficking
A Reality

Rosanna Lyngdoh

Human trafficking is not an issue to be ignored anymore because its implication has great significance. The problem has percolated through to every corner of the world. Survivors of human trafficking are enslaved within a system of subjugation which has far reaching consequence. Even if rescued, the trafficked survivors' dignity and ability to live a normal life is often hindered by society's reluctance to adequately reintegrate them. Human Trafficking is among the most heinous crimes that has relentlessly violated the very essence of human rights.

The most common forms of human trafficking encountered are those of sexual exploitation and forced labour, though other forms also exist. Those who fall victim to human trafficking are often lured to cities and other countries with the promise of employment, marriage or education. These victims are forced into severe exploitation or slavery.

Women and children are the primary victims falling prey to such kind of exploitation but, over the years, a sizable and significant number of male victims are also noticed, especially with reference to forced labour. Trafficking for sexual exploitation and forced labour in overseas employment are in the forefront. Other kinds of human trafficking are hardly reported.

Countries affected by human trafficking can either be a source, destination or transit point. Almost all countries are affected by this predicament. Hence, human trafficking is no longer the problem of developing countries only.

India is a source, a destination and a transit country for men, women and children who fall prey to sex trafficking, forced labour and skilled employment recruitment. Forced labour and sexual exploitation alarmingly accounts for most of the cases.

Though the Government of India through various measures is making significant efforts to curb human trafficking in the country, yet it needs to create stronger measures to eradicate the problem.

There is now a sudden rise of cross border human trafficking in Northeast India over the years. The region is acutely prone to cross border trafficking because of the fact that it shares International borders with Bangladesh, Bhutan, China and Myanmar.

The eight Northeast Indian states of India are connected to the whole of India only through a chicken neck route in Siliguri. Being a region with many conflicts, from insurgency to natural calamities like the yearly floods in Assam, the rate of women and children being trafficked is a vexing problem for the general public and the government.

The problem gets compounded by the heavy and difficult terrain, frequent floods, inadequate job opportunities and the opening of borders for trade and commerce which is porous. The high percentage of people living below the poverty line is the other factor that is increasing the vulnerability of women and children leading to higher incidences in human trafficking. Their vulnerability further increases as they choose to migrate to other states or countries in their search for better job opportunities and livelihood.

Migration for employment, especially for jobs advertised by unregulated agencies increases the chances of people to be highly exploited. Most countries in Middle East and South Asia are best known to be frequented by job seekers, making it easy for dubious employment agencies to lure them.

Trafficked for Prostitution

Farzana (name changed) originally from Assam, comes from an economically poor family. Poverty and domestic violence meted out by male members in her family forced her to work as a domestic helper in Guwahati. She was eventually taken to a Silchar brothel by a known person whereby she was forced into prostitution.

Ranjana T, Geeta T, Sushma T, Padma T (name changed) are all orphans. Because of poverty they were either working as domestic helpers or daily labourers in agricultural fields. The aftermath of the violent earthquake that hit and devastated Nepal in 2016 resulted in some of the girls being lured by traffickers on the pretext of providing jobs in India. These girls were sold to brothels in Silchar.

Fatma, Zeenat, Seema, Resma, Kalpana (names changed) were all orphans forced to work as domestic helpers owing to poverty. They ultimately landed up in brothels after they were trafficked.

Arpana and Anjana (names changed), are sisters, who were married at a very young age, whereafter they were abandoned by their husbands. With no means to support themselves or their children, they met a man in their hometown who promised them jobs. In due course he sold them to a brothel in Silchar.

In early 2015, Impulse NGO Network received an email from an NGO in Nepal stating that there were girls from Nepal who had gone missing after the earthquake and had landed in a brothel in Assam. Impulse NGO Network contacted the Assam Police who then raided the brothel in Silchar and were able to rescue eleven women which included three minor girls from Nepal. All these women and girls were from Assam and Nepal. The women and the three minor girls were produced before the court which passed an order for them to be shifted to Guwahati to shelter-homes for rehabilitation. **(Case Study from Impulse Case Info Centre)**

Until the past two decades, human trafficking was not a well known reality of the region. People were not aware that such a problem existed and no cases were registered.

It was only in 1999 that the general public became aware of the pervasiveness of human trafficking. That year the first case of human trafficking came to light involving three girls from the North East region who were rescued from the brothels of Mumbai by authorities there. They later handed the rescued victims to Impulse NGO Network for their rehabilitation and repatriation.

Major Cities and States of India are recipients of trafficked women and children. Lately though, there has been an increase in demand for young girls in countries like Singapore and the Middle East for the purpose of domestic work; such cases advances to exploitation.

Many unregulated job placement agencies are floating in the country, luring and recruiting people illegally with false promises. Those who are lured often times fall prey to sex trafficking or forced labour.

Unregistered placement agencies play an important role in transporting girls to other countries. Their actions leave no record of the girls' existence in these new countries and the girls are therefore more susceptible to trafficking.

Trafficked through Job Placement

Presently, a plethora of job placement agencies have mushroomed in great numbers offering jobs abroad, some of which are not registered with the governments. They function illegally, luring many unsuspecting young people especially from Northeast India who aspire to work abroad for better pay packages and opportunities.

The easiest way to get jobs in Singapore is by crossing the border from Manipur in India to Myanmar. In 2017, eight girls from Manipur landed up in Yangon, Myanmar. These eight girls were offered jobs by an agent and his accomplice to work as domestic workers in Singapore. The agent and his accomplice took the girls to Yangon, Myanmar, crossing the international border in Manipur. During their stay in Yangon, they were taught how to communicate in English and the local language and also groomed to be presentable. The agents were also processing new passports for them as Burmese citizens.

In no time, during their stay in Yangon, the girls got suspicious and so they contacted their parents in Manipur, who in turn reported the matter to the police.

The police in Manipur contacted the Indian Embassy in Yangon, Myanmar about the missing girls. The Indian Embassy in Yangon with the help of the Anti Trafficking Task Force from Myanmar ultimately rescued the girls. Impulse Case Info Centre Myanmar helped in the rehabilitation and repartriation of the girls back to India.

Impulse Case Info Centre India, New Life Foundation and the Anti Human Trafficking Unit in Manipur later helped the girls to be united with their families after their arrival to Kolkata.

The demand for domestic helpers from Myanmar to Singapore is higher than the demand for domestic helpers from India. Indian citizens are not preferred, but the thirst to work abroad and to earn more wins over the dangers of illegally migrating to another country. It is important to fathom the dangers that lie in smuggling oneself and falling prey to traffickers who are on the lookout for such kind of victims.

(Case Study from Impulse Case Info Centre)

The region is also seeing the sudden rise of women and children being duped into fake marriages and later sold off for prostitution.

A number of skill training institutes under skilling initiatives have swelled up in the region offering a promising future to those who would often fall prey to traffickers, given the vulnerability of their situation.

Another disturbing rising trend is that of girls becoming victims of human trafficking who are lured by dubious men through Social Media sites. The increasing number of girls being duped through such sites is a matter of concern to civil society organizations working on the issue of combating human trafficking.

Trafficked through Social Media Site

Merisha (name changed) aged sixteen, befriended a man on a social media site. For a year, they have been dating on the site even though Merisha had never met him.

One day, Merisha received an email from the man. In the email, it was mentioned that she should come to Bangalore and that a ticket for her travel was attached in the mail. Merisha was overjoyed, as she would finally meet her boyfriend.

Merisha suddenly disappeared from home one day. Her parents searched for her everywhere but she could not be traced.

Meanwhile, Merisha had boarded the flight to Bangalore and reached there. A room was reserved for her in a well known hotel in Bangalore. She was treated well during that period. But at the same time, there was also a discussion between Merisha's boyfriend and some men to take Merisha to another place to meet some people whom she did not know.

Merisha's parents in the meantime had informed the police and Impulse Case Info Centre about her disappearance. The prompt action of the police and the networking organizations saved Merisha from the clutches of the traffickers and she was lucky enough to be rescued. She was brought back home safe and sound.

(Case Study from Impulse Case Info Centre)

Another grave concern is the burgeoning rise of adoption centers in the Northeast India. There are, yet, no records of these adoption centres using unlawful means to adopt children. However, there have been some cases reported of centres in the country illegally giving away children for adoption. There is need, therefore, for the adoption centres to be socially audited and accountable to pre-empt such illegalities.

A 2010 study conducted by Impulse NGO Network revealed that a huge number of children were trafficked for labour. Apparently these children were mostly engaged in the coalmines of Jaintia Hills District of Meghalaya. Many of them were either brought by agents or relatives from neighbouring countries like Nepal and Bangladesh.

Trafficked for Labour

Ram Bahadur (name changed) is from a small village in Nepal. When he was about 12 years of age, he was brought to work in the coal mines in Meghalaya by his neighbour who lives near his place in Nepal.

Ram Bahadur, had never ventured out of his village. He had always craved to see the world outside. When his neighbour told him that he would work in India, he desired to visit India.

Ram Bahadur came to India and landed up in the coal mines of Meghalaya with his neighbour. The rosy picture that his neighbour showed turned out to be a nightmare.

On reaching the coalmines, Ram Bahadur was forced to work in the rat holes, to dig coal. The days turned to years. He was not allowed to talk to anyone. He was given a minimum amount of money. Over the years, he lost contact with his family members.

One day, Ram Bahadur met a man from his village, who had come to work in the coalmines. Ram Bahadur informed him about his family and his desire to meet them.

The man immediately called up some people in Nepal and asked their help to find his family members. His brother-in-law and sister immediately contacted Impulse NGO Network who helped in locating him.

Ram Bahadur was rescued and repatriated back to Nepal in 2015 at the age of 30.

(Case Study from Impulse Case Info Centre)

The issue of human trafficking in the North East of India glaringly indicates that the region needs serious retrospection on this matter. A large percentage of women and children from this region fall prey to traffickers who traffick them to other parts of the country or across borders. The relative simplicity of these people easily allows traffickers to use fraudulent ploys to lure the victims into their web.

Trapped in a Brothel

Jasmine (name changed) age 16 ran away from home to Guwahati because her family forced her to marry a 60 year old man. Upon reaching Guwahati, she loitered about, looking for a job, asking shops and houses if they needed help. She met a man who offered her a job in Siliguri. She instantly accepted the offer and left for Siliguri with him.

On reaching Siliguri, Jasmine was taken to Khalpara, the red light area. There she was sold to a brothel owner. Jasmine was forced to entertain clients more than her body could bear. If she refused, she was beaten and tortured.

A man (name withheld) who often visits the brothel came in contact with Jasmine and informed Impulse Case Info Centre about her.

Impulse Case Info Centre sought the help of Police department (AHTU) of Meghalaya, Assam, West Bengal and finally the girl was rescued.

Many women and children are forced into such kinds of trade either by force or fraudulent means. A sizable number of people especially women and children, are sold off in red light area.

Every other day, ICIC India receives an average of three human trafficking cases.

(Case Study from Impulse Case Info Centre)

There have been efforts to organize programs and create awareness throughout the region to combat trafficking. Yet, the number of trafficking cases is increasing. NGOs, Faith-based organizations and government agencies are making efforts to educate the masses on human trafficking, though this has yet to manifest in a decrease in trafficking cases. The low rate of conviction or prosecution seems to communicate to traffickers that the criminal industry is worth the risk.

With the rescue of the three girls in 1999 by the authorities in Mumbai, who later handed the girls to Impulse NGO Network for their rehabilitation and repatriation, there is an urge to educate the region about human trafficking. The NGO, over time, has fostered awareness about the problem, and has merged with various government departments, NGOs, Media Houses and Law Enforcement agencies to support their efforts to combat human trafficking.

Often times, unsafe migration of people to different cities and states due to poverty, lack of job opportunities and livelihood have made them more exposed to unwanted exploitation.

The stark reality of human trafficking will prevail and people will still be exploited until the issue of unsafe migration and livelihood is addressed.

5

Human Trafficking vis-a-vis Legal Provisions and Enforcement

Tongpang L. Jamir

Introduction

Irrefutable is the fact that trafficking in human beings is one of the largest organized crimes across the world, along with trafficking in drugs and arms. And, undoubtedly, it is as much a commercial activity as an organized crime. The scourge of 'human trafficking' needs no introduction. Every year, millions of individuals are trafficked all over the world and are coerced into living conditions that amount to slavery, forced labour and servitude. Since innumerable young girls and women are especially victimized by trafficking, this problem is seen as one that intersects with that of commercial sexual exploitation. In particular, the trafficking of women and children has received the attention of governments all over the world as well as at a multilateral level. It has been clearly denounced by the international community as a blatant violation of human rights, a modern form of slavery, and a particularly heinous form of violence against women. From the legal point of view - India has been a front-runner in the battle against human trafficking. The criminalization of trafficking flows from Article 23 (1) of the Constitution which states that – "Traffic in human beings and 'beggar' and other similar forms of forced labour are prohibited and any contravention of this provision shall be an offence punishable in accordance with law". To tackle human trafficking, we have had the necessary legislation in place, principally the Immoral Traffic (Prevention) Act, 1956, in addition to several provisions in labour laws and the Indian Penal Code. These form a composite legal code for the prosecution and punishment of traffickers. In addition to these legislative measures, the Supreme Court of India has touched on this issue in two prominent judgments, i.e., – Vishal Jeet v., Union of India (1990) and in Gaurav Jain v., Union of India (1997). These judgments directed the Government of India, among other things, to prepare a 'National Plan to Combat Trafficking and Commercial Sexual Exploitation of Women and Children'. As a result of this, a National Plan was drafted in 1998 which lays down suggested measures for prevention, rescue, rehabilitation and reintegration.

Myths Versus Reality of Trafficking

Sr. No	Myths	Reality/Truths
1.	Trafficking in human beings is only done for prostitution. Prostitution is only one of the reasons for trafficking.	Prostitution is only one of the reasons for trafficking. Trafficking is done for various purposes, such as begging, forced labour, debt bondage, illicit adoption, marriage, organ transplant, camel jockeying, for performance in circus, for child sex – tourism, and for use of adults and children in pornography.
2.	'Human smuggling' or 'voluntary illegal migration' is the same as trafficking in human beings.	**Human smuggling** - is the facilitation, transportation, attempted transportation or illegal entry of a person(s) across an international border, in violation of one or more countries' laws, either clandestinely or through deception, such as the use of fraudulent documents.

		Human trafficking - unlike smuggling, which is often a criminal commercial transaction between two willing parties who go their separate ways once their business is complete, trafficking specifically targets the trafficked person as an object of criminal exploitation. The purpose from the beginning of the trafficking enterprise is to profit from the exploitation of the victim. It follows that fraud, force or coercion all play a major role in trafficking.
3.	In trafficking for prostitution, the brothel manager/ madam is the main accused in a trafficking crime.	Brothel manager/madam is only the visible face of the exploiter and trafficker is the main culprit.
4.	Brothel is the only scene of crime in trafficking.	The scene of crime in trafficking involves all places in of crime in trafficking. Source, Transit and Destination. It includes places where exploitation takes place under the facade of other enterprises, such as beauty and massage parlours, friendship clubs, small hotels, exclusive clubs, under the guise of call centres, friendship clubs, and along national highways, etc.
5.	The law to address trafficking is only ITPA.	Trafficking for CSE has to be addressed by invoking not trafficking is not only ITPA. Only ITPA but relevant provisions of IPC (ex. 366 A, 366 B, 372, 373, 375, 376, etc.,).
6.	All women seen to be soliciting are accused persons under ITPA.	Case studies and research shows that most of these women are made to solicit by the exploiters; there is no mens-rea and these women are victims.
7.	Customer is not an accused under ITPA.	Customer is culpable under S. 5 (1) (d) and 7 (1) ITPA and related IPC offences.

8.	Only a Special Police Officer can arrest a trafficking accused.	Any officer of the rank of SI and above can be authorized under ITPA by a Special Police officer, in writing (S. 14 (ii)) or otherwise (S. 14 (iii)). However, any person committing or likely to commit a cognizable offence can be arrested by any police officer, including a constable. (S. 41 Cr. PC).
9.	Without FIR no arrest or rescue is possible.	Trafficking being a cognizable offence, any police officer can cause arrest or rescue even without FIR to prevent crime (S. 41 Cr. PC). Moreover a Magistrate can authorize any police officer of the rank of SI and above for carrying out rescue (S. 16 (1) of ITPA).
10.	A PO can register a case of trafficking only after rescue.	Rescue normally takes place at the point of final destination, whereas trafficking offences commence at the source itself and continues through transit to the destination point and even thereafter. If PO gets information about any person having been transferred from source point or being trafficked through transit place, the PO of those areas should register FIR for the offence of trafficking u/S. 5 (3) of ITPA.

Dynamics of Trafficking in India

Human trafficking has, over the last few decades, become one of the most lucrative forms of organized crimes across the globe. The buying and selling of persons for the purpose of sexual exploitation, forced labour, domestic work and organ trade has become common. India for long has been considered the source, destination and transit country for women and children for forced labour and sex-trafficking. In India, 90% of trafficking occurs domestically (intra-state or inter-state), and 10% occurs across national borders. The country serves as a destination for persons trafficked from neighbouring countries such as Nepal and Bangladesh, and as a transit country for individuals being trafficked to the Middle East and other parts of the world. In addition, India is a source country for individuals trafficked to Europe, the Middle East and North America. The majority of trafficked persons in India, including men, women, boys and girls, are trafficked for purposes of forced labour. Labour trafficking is the trafficking of a person by means of fraud, coercion or duress for the purpose of exploiting him or her for forced labour or services or slavery or practices similar to slavery, including involuntary servitude, peonage and debt bondage. Sex trafficking is also prevalent within India and predominantly affects women and girls. Sex trafficking is the trafficking of a person by means of fraud, coercion or duress for the purpose of exploiting him or her for involuntary commercial sex acts, prostitution of that person or other forms of sexual exploitation

- The most prevalent sectors employing victims of TIP in India are for commercial sex work; bonded labour, (i.e., in both the industrial and agricultural sectors); domestic work; Entertainment (circuses, camel Jockeying) and begging. Commercial sex work and labour accounts form a large share of trafficking.
- The main cause of trafficking in India is poverty. Poor individuals that engage in migrant labour are particularly susceptible to the manipulation of traffickers when false jobs are promised, and women are easily allured by the attraction of fake marriage as a way of escaping poverty. Those states with the highest levels of poverty are where the largest numbers of victims of trafficking originate (e.g. Orissa, Bihar, Jharkhand, Chhattisgarh, and West Bengal). Poverty's impact on trafficking is amplified by the impact of globalization on both poor and wealthy areas of the country.
- Social practices and cultural factors such as patriarchal bias, low regard for women's rights, low level of girls' education, marginalization of women, and the dowry practice negatively influence trafficking almost as much as poverty. Many families and communities perpetuate

and institutionalize (e.g., through traditional practices) the act of trafficking. One study indicated that 62% of women in commercial sex work were from scheduled castes and 30% were from scheduled tribes. In addition to being historically disenfranchised, these groups are known for several cultural practices that are adverse to women.

- Lesser, but still important, root causes for trafficking in India are conflicts/natural disasters and governance. Orissa's cyclones and rebel groups in Jharkhand and Chhattisgarh have all contributed to an increase trafficking. Despite the existence of legislation, poor implementation and information asymmetries ensure that marginalized segments vulnerable to trafficking are not aware of, or able to access protection through the law. Migration policies that are especially harsh on unskilled workers, forcing them to resort to alternative livelihood options through illegal means.
- On the demand side, globalization and economic booms have increased the demand for sex workers and cheap labour, leading to a resultant increase in the supply of trafficked victims, especially in Delhi and Goa. Both low levels and high levels of economic development can encourage trafficking, implying that states can transition from being sources to destinations as they develop economically. There are very few efforts to address the demand side of trafficking.
- Trafficking has social, economic and health impacts. Trafficking re-enforces discriminatory behaviour and, in terms of the lost potential returns to human capital, economic losses from human trafficking to communities are enormous. Finally, victims, especially those engaged in sex work, are highly vulnerable to HIV/AIDS, malaria, tuberculosis, and other diseases.

India's Legal Obligations and the United Nations Trafficking Protocol

Human trafficking is an egregious human rights violation that occurs throughout the world. Due to its complex cross-border nature, human trafficking requires a coordinated, multi-disciplinary National and International response. The United Nations Protocol to Prevent, Suppress and Punish Trafficking in Persons, Especially Women and Children (the UN Trafficking Protocol) provide a roadmap for cross national collaboration as well as recommendations for enacting effective domestic human trafficking laws. In May 2011, India ratified the three protocols of the United Nations Convention against Transnational Organized Crime, including the UN Trafficking Protocol.

A. **The UN Trafficking Protocol:** The UN Trafficking Protocol provides a comprehensive framework for addressing the trafficking of persons internationally and domestically. The Protocol's definition of human trafficking delineates the wide variety of conduct constituting the crime of trafficking persons. Under this definition, a person is guilty of the crime of human trafficking if they satisfy three components: (1) an act (e.g., transportation, or receipt of persons), (2) by a specified means (e.g., threat or use of force or other forms of coercion, abduction, fraud, etc.), (3) resulting in "exploitation," as defined by the Protocol. Exploitation is defined as "including, at a minimum, the exploitation of the prostitution of others, or other forms of sexual exploitation, forced labour or services, slavery or similar practices, servitude, or the removal of organs." The UN Trafficking Protocol obligates States to criminalize trafficking in persons, to take steps to prevent human trafficking, and to assist, protect and repatriate victims of human trafficking safely.

B. **India's Obligation To Uphold The UN Trafficking Protocol:** Almost a decade after signing the United Nations Convention Against Transnational Organized Crime (UNTOC), India officially ratified the Convention and its three Protocols, including the UN Trafficking Protocol on May 5, 2011. The process of ratification formally indicated the State's consent to be bound by the terms and provisions of the UNTOC and its Protocols. However, India has a dualist regime with regard to International law and International Treaties. This means that, according to the Indian Constitution, ratified treaties do not automatically have the force of law in domestic courts. However, the Indian Constitution states that the Government of India must adhere to its treaty obligations and "endeavor to…foster respect for International law treaty obligations in the dealings of organized peoples with one another." In addition, the Indian Supreme Court declared that the Constitution itself must be interpreted in light of any international treaties that India has ratified. In addition, the Supreme Court in *Vishaka v. Rajasthan* established that provisions of International Treaties might be read into existing Indian law in order to "expand" their protections. Moreover, in the absence of Domestic law, "the contents of International Conventions and norms are significant for the purpose of interpretation." Thus, although India has not expressly incorporated the entirety of the UN Trafficking Protocol into its National law, the Indian Government is nonetheless required to adhere to all of its obligations under the Protocol. Moreover, in line with the judicial precedents discussed above, the anti-trafficking provisions of the Indian Constitution, Penal Code, and other Domestic Legislation should be interpreted in light of the UN Trafficking Protocol and other International Treaties to which India is a party.

Constitutional and Legal Provisions in India and Enforcement of the Laws

Constitution and Substantive laws like the Indian Penal Code 1860, special legislations like the Immoral Traffic (Prevention) Act 1956, the Bonded Labour System (Abolition) Act 1976, etc., and local laws like the Goa Children's Act 2003, provide the legal regime to combat and prevent Human Trafficking (HT). In addition, judgments by the Supreme Court and various High Courts have provided further legal strength to the law enforcement agencies.

1. Constitutional Provision

The Constitution of India vide Article 23 (1) prohibits both trafficking in human beings and forced labour. Trafficking in human beings has been prevalent in India for a long time in the form of prostitution and selling and purchasing of human beings.

Article 23 (1) Traffic in human beings and beggar and other similar forms of forced labour are prohibited and any contravention of this provision shall be an offence punishable in accordance with law. Article 23 (2) Nothing in this article shall prevent the State from imposing compulsory service for public purposes, and in imposing such service the State shall not make any discrimination on grounds only of religion, race, caste or class or any of them.

2. Amendment to The Indian Penal Code and Inclusion of Definition of Trafficking (Section 370 in 2013)

Following a horrific gang rape of a woman in New Delhi in 2012, a Committee was constituted on 23 December 2012. It was set up under the chairpersonship of Justice Verma to review laws on sexual assault and give recommendations. Based on the recommendations of what is popularly known as the Justice Verma Committee Report, a definition of trafficking was added to the IPC in its amendment in 2013.

Section 370 of IPC:

Whoever, for the purpose of exploitation, (a) recruits (b) transports (c) harbours (d) transfers or (e) receives, a person or persons by —

Firstly threats, or
Secondly using force or any other form of coercion, or
Thirdly by abduction, or
Fourthly by practicing fraud or deception, or
Fifthly by abuse of power, or

Sixthly by inducement, including by giving or receiving of payments or benefits, in order to achieve the consent of any person having control over the person recruited, transported, harboured, transferred or received; commits the offence of trafficking. While the law in its entirety is applicable to children too, the explanations to this section include some very specific mention of children or minors:

1. The expression "exploitation" shall include any act of physical exploitation or any form of sexual exploitation, slavery or practices similar to slavery, servitude, or the forced removal of organs.
2. The consent of the victim is immaterial in determination of the offence of trafficking.
3. Whoever commits the offence of trafficking shall be punished with rigorous imprisonment for a term which shall not be less than seven years, but which may extend to ten years, and shall also be liable to fine.
4. Where the offence involves the trafficking of more than one person, it shall be punishable with rigorous imprisonment for a term which shall not be less than ten years but which may extend to imprisonment for life, and shall also be liable to fine.
5. Where the offence **involves the trafficking of a minor**, it shall be punishable with rigorous imprisonment for a term which shall not be less than ten years, but which may extend to imprisonment for life, and shall also be liable to fine.
6. Where the offence involves **the trafficking of more than one minor,** it shall be punishable with rigorous imprisonment for a term which shall not be less than fourteen years, but which may extend to imprisonment for life, and shall also be liable to fine.
7. If a person is convicted of the offence of **trafficking of minor** on more than one occasion, then such person shall be punished with imprisonment for life, which shall mean imprisonment for the remainder of that person's natural life, and shall also be liable to fine.

8. When a public servant or a police officer is involved in the trafficking of any person then, such public servant or police officer shall be punished with imprisonment for life, which shall mean imprisonment for the remainder of that person's natural life, and shall also be liable to fine.

3. Juvenile Justice (Care and Protection of Children) Act, 2015

The JJ Act 2000 was one of the most comprehensive Acts to deal with the issue of children and this Act also provides a universal definition of the child as 'any person below the age of 18 years'. To address the issues of children with greater sensitivity, the Act separates children into two broader categories:

1. Children in need of care and protection
2. Children in conflict with law (child in conflict with law means a child who is alleged or found to have committed an offence and who has not completed eighteen years of age on the date of commission of such offence).

The JJ Act identifies certain offences as special offences against children and addresses the crime of trafficking of children for beggary and labour and in general provides for cruelty against children by persons having their charge or control over them. Besides mentioning children who are trafficked categorically as those who are in need of care and protection, the JJ Act 2015, also included several other categories of children who could be already trafficked children or are in situations that make them vulnerable to trafficking (Section 14): who is found working in contravention of labour laws for the time being in force or is found begging, or living on the street; or has threatened to kill, injure, exploit or abuse the child and there is a reasonable likelihood of the threat being carried out; who is missing or run away child, or whose parents cannot be found after making reasonable inquiry in such manner as may be prescribed; or who has been or is being or is likely to be abused, tortured or exploited for the purpose of sexual abuse or illegal acts; or who is found vulnerable and is likely to be inducted into drug abuse or **trafficking**; or who is being or is likely to be abused for unconscionable gains; or who is victim of or affected by any armed conflict, civil unrest or natural calamity; or who is at imminent risk of marriage before attaining the age of marriage and whose parents, family members, guardian and any other persons are likely to be responsible for solemnisation of such marriage. In addition, the JJ Act recognises sale and procurement of children for any purpose as a cognizable and non-bailable offence with punishment of rigorous imprisonment that may extend to five years and shall also be liable to a fine of one lakh rupees. It also prohibits the use of children for begging, vending, peddling or smuggling of drugs and psychotropic substances, for labour, as child combatant by non-state, self styled militant groups and for illegal adoption.

4. Code of Criminal Procedure

Responsibility for providing compensation to trafficking victims is fragmented between the Central Government and individual States. This is largely the result of Section 357, Code of Criminal Procedure, which states that the Central Government should be responsible for compensating victims of any crime (not limited to trafficking) who have suffered loss or injury. According to the Section:

"(1) When a Court imposes a sentence of fine or a sentence (including a sentence of death) of which fine forms a part, the Court may, when passing judgment order the whole or any part of the fine recovered to be applied .

(2) In the payment to any person of compensation for any loss or injury caused by the offence, which compensation is, the opinion of the Court, recoverable by such person in a Civil Court . . ."

The Section addresses the compensation of trafficking victims; however, it allows for the individual State's determination of compensation procedures and amounts. As a result, there is no centralized compensatory system for trafficking victims in India. The Centrally Sponsored Rehabilitation Scheme for Bonded Labour mandates a rehabilitation grant of Rs. 20,000/- to each bonded labourer as well as assistance for rehabilitation.

5. Protection of Children from Sexual Offences Act, 2012 (POCSO Act)

POCSO ACT 2012 was implemented in India to strengthen the legal provisions for the protection of children from sexual abuse and exploitation. For the first time, a special law has been passed to address the issue of sexual offences against children which is also gender specific. Sexual offences were earlier covered under different sections of the Indian Penal Code. But, the IPC did not expressly provide for all types of sexual offences against children and, more importantly, it does not distinguish between adult and child victims. IPC is not gender specific as well. However, POCSO Act provides stringent punishments, which have been categorized as per the gravity of the offence. The punishments range from simple to rigorous imprisonment of varying degrees. There is also a provision of fine which needs to be decided as per the discretion of the Court.

The Various Offences Clearly Outlined in this Act Are

1. **Penetrative Sexual Assault (Section 3):** Penetration which is peno-vaginal, peno-urethral or peno-anal, fingering or object penetration come under the category of this offence. The minimum punishment prescribed for this offence is 7 years and maximum punishment prescribed for this offence can extend till life term imprisonment accompanied with fine **(Section 4).**
2. **Aggravated Penetrative Sexual Assault (Section 5):** Any of the offences covered in the penetrative sexual assault section, if committed by a person of trust or authority such as a police officer, teacher, parent, care giver then the offences become aggravated penetrative sexual assault. The minimum punishment prescribed for this offence is 10 years and maximum punishment prescribed for this offence can extend till life term imprisonment accompanied with fine **(Section 6).**
3. **Non-Penetrative Sexual Assault (Section 7):** Whoever commits this offence with sexual intent, like touching the

vagina, penis, anus or breast of the child; forces or makes the child touch the vagina, penis, anus or breast of such person does any act with sexual intent which involves physical contact without penetration is guilty of offence covered in this section. The minimum punishment prescribed for this offence is 3 years and maximum punishment prescribed for this offence is 5 years accompanied with fine **(Section 8).**

4. **Aggravated Sexual Assault (Section 9):** Any of the offences coved in the non-penetrative sexual offences section if committed by a person of trust or authority such as a police officer, teacher, parent, care giver then the offences falls under this category of offences. The minimum punishment prescribed for this offence is 5 years and maximum punishment prescribed for this offence is 7 years accompanied with fine **(Section 10).**
5. **Sexual Harassment of Children (Section 11):** Any unwelcome sexual remarks, gestures, emails, telephone calls, taunting, jeering, demands or requests for sexual favours amounts to sexual harassment. The maximum punishment prescribed for this offence is 3 years accompanied with fine **(Section 12).**
6. **Use of Child for Pornographic Purpose (Section 13):** Any offence which involves a child in the preparation, distribution, production, marketing, and or distribution of pornography via computer, internet, sprint, electronic or any other technology attracts this offence. The minimum punishment prescribed for this offence is 5 years with fine and in the event of subsequent conviction punishment can extend till 7 years with fine **(Section 14 (1).**
7. **Attempt to Commit an Offence** is also punishable with a sentence of 1 year and fine in POCSO **(Section 18).**
8. **Abetment of Offence:** Intentionally aiding an offence or instigating a person to commit an offence is also punishable under POCSO. The punishment for abetment of offence is similar as that provided for the offence itself.

9. **Failure to Report an Offence:** It is mandatory requirement to report an offence and the failure to report an offence is also made punishable in POCSO. The punishment prescribed for failure to report is 6 month and or a fine **(Section 21).**

6. Prohibition of Child Marriage Act, 2006 (PCMA)

Although, this law is essentially about prohibiting child marriage, recognising that there is a lot trafficking for and through marriage, it categorically states that a child marriage is recognised as invalid and hence null and void especially where some of the following means are used for the purpose of marriage –

use of force or,
inducement or,
kidnapping or,
sale or,
trafficking or,

If after the marriage the child bride is sold or trafficked for immoral purposes, then such marriage is also held invalid and declared null and void.

If an adult male who is above 18 years of age contracts **child marriage**, he shall be punishable with rigorous imprisonment for 2 years or with fine which may extend to one lakh rupees or both.

7. National Policy for Children, 2013

The State shall protect all children from all forms of violence and abuse, harm, neglect, stigma, discrimination, deprivation, exploitation including economic exploitation and sexual exploitation, abandonment, separation, abduction, **sale or trafficking for any purpose or in any form**, pornography, alcohol and substance abuse, or any other activity that takes undue advantage of them, or harms their personhood or affects their development.

8. India's Bonded Labour System (Abolition) Act, 1976

Punishment for enforcement of bonded labour.-

Section 16. Whoever, after the commencement of this Act, compels any person to render any bonded labour shall be punishable with imprisonment for a term which may extend to three years and also with fine which may extend to two thousand rupees.

Section 17. Punishment for advancement of bonded debt: imprisonment for a term which may extend to three years and also with fine which may extend to two thousand rupees.

Section 18. Punishment for extracting bonded labour under the bonded labour system.- punishable with imprisonment for a term which may extend to three years and also with fine which may extend to two thousand rupees.

Section 19. Punishment for omission or failure to restore possession of property to bonded labourers.- punishable with imprisonment for a term which may extend to one year, or with fine which may extend to one thousand rupees, or with both.

Section 20. Abetment to be an offence.- punishable with the same punishment as is provided for the offence which has been abetted.

9. Sections 366 (A) and 372 IPC

Prohibits kidnapping and selling minors into prostitution respectively. Penalties under these provisions are a maximum of 10 years imprisonment and fine.

10. Transplantation of Human Organs Act, 1994

Punishment for removal of human organ without authority:

(1) Any person who renders his services to or any hospital and who, for purposes of transplantation, conducts, associates with, or help in any manner in, the removal of any human organ without authority, shall be punishable with imprisonment for a term which may extend to five years and with fine which may extend to ten thousand rupees.

(2) Where any person convicted under sub-section (1) is a registered medical practitioner, his name shall be reported by the Appropriate Authority to the respective State Medical Council for taking necessary action including the removal of his name from the register of the Council for a period

of two years for the first offence and permanently for the subsequent offence.

Punishment for commercial dealings in human organs:

Whoever —

(a) makes or receives any payment for the supply of, or for an offer to supply, any human organ;

(b) seeks to find a person willing to supply for payment any human organ;

(c) offers to supply any human organ for payment;

(d) initiates or negotiates any arrangement involving the making of any payment for the supply of, or for an offer to supply, any human organ;

(e) takes part in the management or control of a body of persons, whether a society, firm or company, whose activities consist of or include the initiation or negotiation of any arrangement referred to in clause (d); or;

(f) publishes or distributes or causes to be published or distributed any advertisement, —

  (a) inviting persons to supply for payment of any human organ;

  (b) offering to supply any human organ for payment; or

  (c) indicating that the advertiser is willing to initiate or negotiate any arrangement referred to in clause (d), shall be punishable with imprisonment for a term which shall not be less than two years but which may extend to seven years and shall be liable to fine which shall not be less than ten thousand rupees but may extend to twenty thousand rupees;

Provided that the court may, for any adequate and special reason to be mentioned in the judgment, impose a sentence of imprisonment for a term of less than two years and a fine less than ten thousand rupees.

Some Landmark Judgments

1. **Court Rules that advocates appearing for pimps and brothel owners cannot appear for the victim**
   Prerna v. State of Maharashtra [2003 (2) Mah. L. J. 105
2. **Guidelines for search of missing children laid down by the Supreme Court**
   Hori Lal v. Commissioner of Police, Delhi & Ors. Respondents [Writ Petition (Crl.) No. 610/1996]
3. **"Prostitution" per se is not an offence and prostitutes should not be harassed by police**
   Radha & Ors. v. State of UP [2003 (1) AWC 455]
4. **"Detention" under Section 6 to be interpreted widely and consent is not material**
   Nilofar & Nilam Usman Sheikh v. State of Gujarat [(2004) 3 GLR 2630]
5. **Sealing of brothels will ensure the curbing of organised crime**
   Geeta Kancha Tamang v. State of Maharashtra [Criminal Appeal No. 858 of 2009]
6. **Decisions of the Child Welfare Committee are final in terms of care and protection of children**
   Munni v. State of Maharashtra [Criminal Writ Petition No. 227/2011(Bombay High Court)]
7. **Supreme Court issued directives for registration of FIRs in cases of missing children**
   Bachpan Bachao Andolan v. Union of India & Others [Writ Petition Civil 75/ 2012]
8. **Supreme Court appoints a panel to monitor and suggest rehabilitation scheme for trafficked sex workers and trafficked victims**
   Budhadev Karmaskar v. State of West Bengal, [(2011) 11 SCC 538]
9. **Children at railway stations**
   Khushboo Jain v. Ministry of Railways [Writ Petition (Civil) 5365 of 2012, Delhi High Court]

Some Important Schemes

Ujjawala: A Comprehensive Scheme for Prevention of Trafficking and Rescue, Rehabilitation and Re-Integration of Victims of Trafficking for Commercial Sexual Exploitation.

The *Ujjawala:* A Comprehensive Scheme for Prevention of Trafficking and Rescue, Rehabilitation and Re-Integration of Victims of Trafficking for Commercial Sexual Exploitation, under the Ministry for Women and Child Development, attempts to "provide rehabilitation services both immediate and long-term to the victims by providing basic amenities/needs such as shelter, food, clothing, medical treatment including counselling, legal aid and guidance and vocational training." The *Ujjawala* Scheme provides victims with funding to meet the travel costs incurred en route to being restored with their families, as well as "seed money" of Rs. 5,000/- to each victim.

Swadhar Greh: A Scheme for Women In Difficult Circumstances

A Scheme for Women in Difficult Circumstances, also under the Ministry of Women and Child Development, represents another such programme. The *Swadhar Greh* Scheme is meant "to provide temporary accommodation, maintenance and rehabilitative services to women and girls rendered homeless due to family discord, crime, violence, mental stress, social ostracism or [who] are being forced into prostitution and are in mortal danger." Beneficiaries of the *Swadhar Greh* Scheme include "trafficked women/girls rescued or runaway from brothels or other places where they face exploitation." Both schemes, however, only apply to persons trafficked for the purposes of sexual exploitation.

NALSA (Victims of Trafficking and Commercial Sexual Exploitation) Scheme, 2015

Legal Services to Victims of Trafficking and Commercial Sexual Exploitation: Trafficking of women and children for commercial sexual exploitation is an organized crime and is said to be the most lucrative trade or business after arms and narcotics. Most of the time, innocent women and children, as young as nine years old, are pushed into this trade by people known to them, including their own families. Once in the trade, the victim has no escape route and has to languish on an environment of violence, abuse and exploitation.

The primary objective of the Scheme is to provide legal assistance against trafficking and sexual exploitation. Within its wide ambit, the Scheme covers children, adolescent girls and women of all ages. The Scheme seeks to provide an action plan to prevent sexual exploitation of these individuals while ensuring rescue and rehabilitation of the victims of trafficking and voluntary sex workers.

Action Plan: To coordinate with State, Govt./Non-governmental agencies and organizations to ensure that the benefits of all legislations, policies and schemes of the government reach the exploited persons and effective preventive and rehabilitative measures are initiated at the ground level. The Legal Services Authorities shall create awareness amongst the vulnerable groups with a view to empowering them to demand and avail their entitlements. The Authorities shall work for capacity building of all stakeholders including those in the law enforcing and justice delivery system for them to effectively deal with the issues concerning trafficked and sexually exploited women and children.

Measures Taken By Government To Combat Human Trafficking

1. Ministry of Home Affairs, Government of India
2. Ministry of Women and Child Development, Government of India
3. Ministry of Overseas Indian Affairs, Government of India
4. Ministry of Labour and Employment, Government of India
5. National Commission for Protection of Child Rights (NCPCR)
6. IGNOU Course on Human Trafficking
7. Anti Human Traffic Units
8. Strengthening Capacity Building
9. Judicial Colloquiums

Way Forward

1. Increase prosecutions and convictions for all forms of trafficking, including forced and bonded labour, and of officials allegedly complicit in trafficking, respecting due process;
2. establish and fully resource anti-human trafficking units (AHTUs) in all districts, including by providing additional dedicated, trained staff and by clarifying the mandate of AHTUs;
3. develop and implement standard operating procedures (SOPs) to harmonize victim identification and referral, and train officials on their use;
4. address jurisdictional issues in the investigation of suspected traffickers and use of testimony when trafficking crimes cross state lines;
5. cease the penalization of trafficking victims; protect victim confidentiality and privacy, including on government-issued identification documents;
6. develop and adopt a national action plan to combat trafficking;
7. improve central and state government implementation of protection programs and compensation schemes to ensure trafficking victims receive benefits, release certificates, and compensation funds;
8. take steps to eliminate all recruitment fees charged to workers;
9. promptly disburse government funding for shelters and develop monitoring mechanisms to ensure quality of care;
10. continue to increase the transparency of government efforts to combat trafficking and provide disaggregated data on efforts to criminally investigate, prosecute, and punish sex and labour;
11. trafficking;
12. provide funding for states to establish fast-track courts that deal with all forms of human trafficking;

13. and provide anti-trafficking training or guidance for diplomatic personnel to prevent their engagement in or facilitation of trafficking crimes,
14. and to provide personnel the tools to identify and assist trafficking victims in their work.

Conclusion

There is little reason to dispute the fact that there has been a lot of progress in the understanding of the concept of trafficking as well in the interventions made to address the issue in the last decade. But, as consumerism (the result of globalisation and markets opening up) gains momentum, the nature and purposes of trafficking are mounting as are the number of children being trafficked. While the campaign (till 2012) was to build a more holistic understanding of the problem of trafficking, the next few years need to be spent in monitoring the implementation of the law as well in providing support to the infrastructures and institutions created to address trafficking.

Gathering and managing data has been an intractable problem, and continues to remain so. As migration patterns increase and get closely intertwined with issues of trafficking, it is important that the challenge of estimating numbers of children and women trafficked be handled. There is need to estimate the numbers of children and women trafficked with a fair degree of accuracy for interventions to be effective. Patriarchy (and the trend of son preference) is a persistent problem and has become endemic. The falling sex ratios are evidence of it. This is particularly true in the northern states where the problems of the trafficking of girls have increased. Attitudinal change and the involvement of a whole range of actors in societies are needed to tackle these challenges. Laws, policies, protocols, Standard Operating Procedures (SOPs) will remain inadequate in addressing the problem unless backed by adequate financial resources.

Since, trafficking is a complicated and multifaceted problem; it requires a co-ordinated and inter-disciplinary response. It touches on the domains of 'human rights protection' and 'gender justice' while posing some difficult problems for law-enforcement officials. There is of course an urgent need for intensified action to curb this menace. I hope that the participants of this seminar will develop a 'Plan of Action' for themselves in improving justice delivery and tackling the problem of 'human trafficking' in the country. It is hoped that a proper reading of the law will lead to its better enforcement; victims will be rescued more effectively, appropriate protective measures will be ordered with due regard to the age of the victims and they will have a better chance of reintegration in society.

6

Biblical Response to Human Trafficking

A. Tali Ao

Introduction

Slavery takes different forms. Human trafficking is one of such forms which can severely damage and destroy often irrecoverably the core of human dignity and destiny, and life itself. This problem is thus known as modern slavery. By its very nature, it consists of combination of myriads of criminal acts and breach of fundamental human rights. It is an appalling traumatic experience for the victims and their love ones, and it is a huge social problem which has far-reaching destructive consequences for those persons involved, the survivors, their families and the immediate social environment, and the society at large. This presentation is an attempt to give a brief overview of what the Bible has to say on and against this problem and to indicate the essential faith resources to back up individuals and agencies in their fight and hope to eradicate the crime and in their effort to combat this menace and rescue, and restore victims caught up in the crime.

Definition

According to the United Nations Convention against transnational organized crime, article three of the Protocol to Prevent, Suppress and Punish Trafficking in Persons, Especially Women and Children, human trafficking is defined as: "the recruitment, transportation, transfer, harboring or receipt of persons, by means of the threat or use of force or other forms of coercion, of abduction, of fraud, of deception, of the abuse of power or of a position of vulnerability, or of the giving or receiving of payments or benefits to achieve the consent of a person having control over another person, for the purpose of exploitation. Exploitation shall include, at a minimum, the exploitation of the prostitution of others or other forms of sexual exploitation, forced labour or services, slavery or practices similar to slavery, servitude or the removal of organs."[1]

Life as a Divine Gift

The core concern of the above definition is the safeguarding of life from abuse, commoditization of persons leading to pain and suffering, injury, disappearance and eventually death. In tune with such concerns several laws and teachings are enshrined in the Bible which are relevant and authoritative, and have in many ways informed and influenced modern moral teachings, conventions, declarations and state laws and law makers that are intended to prevent human trafficking and protect the sanctity and dignity of life. According to biblical teaching the most precious gift of God to the world and humanity is the life. The deadly tentacles of human trafficking directly and indirectly destroy, diminish and maim this precious gift either permanently or temporarily and rob the quality of life or fullness of life of a person. It also threatens other areas of life and its support systems for healthy life and peaceful co-existence.

Within the creation narrative, Genesis 2:7 is the classic text with regard to idea of giving of life in the Old Testament (OT). It portrays the LORD God *inbreathing* into the human's nostrils *the breath of life*, as a result, the human became a *living* being. The

1 Irena Koričanac, "Human Trafficking, Trauma and Psychotherapy: Conclusions and Recommendations from the International Conference - Contemporary Psycho-Social Challenges in Combating Human Trafficking," in Irena Koričanac, ed., *Human Trafficking Trauma and Psychotherapy Collection of Paper* (Belgrade: ASTRA, 2013), 16.

key idea in this passage is that life in general, and life of humans in particular, is the gift of God and that humans arose as a group of living beings. The use of the title, "Yahweh Elohim" expresses the author's conviction that Yahweh is not merely Israel's national deity but the sovereign God who rules over and controls all things and is the ultimate Lord, owner of life, and judge of all.[2]

Human Beings as Crown of God's Creation

The most crucial element of human life is his/her dignity and modesty which are battered and put into great danger in human trafficking. Within the OT wisdom literature, the psalmist affirms that human being is the crown of God's creation. The relevant passage says:

> When I look at your heavens, the work of your fingers, the moon and the stars that you have established; what are human beings that you are mindful of them, mortals that you care for them? Yet you have made them a little lower than God, and crowned them with glory and honor (Psalm 8:3-5).

Further the palmist praises the Creator saying, "I praise you, for I am fearfully and wonderfully made" (Psalm 139:14). In the ordeals of trafficking not only his/her dignity but all aspects of the victim's life, especially the vital organs, are put into great danger if not permanently destroyed or stolen if the victim was trafficked for organ trading.

Spirit of Yahweh as the Source of Life

Another important aspect of the OT thought related with the ideas of giving of life is the notion that the Spirit of Yahweh as the source of life. Just as natural life is created through God's gift of a natural spirit so the divine eternal life came about through the infusion of the Spirit. Besides Genesis 2:7, Ezekiel 37:4-10 also talk about God breathing breath of life and the image of Yahweh as giving life to 'dry bones' through the infusion of the Spirit. The Spirit of Yahweh, compared often to the wind as the source

---

2 G. J. Wenham, *Genesis 1-15*, WBC, vol. I (Dallas, Texas: Word Books, 1987), 60.

of life was an ancient concept in Israel as well as the doctrine of a pouring forth of the Spirit in the eschatological times. The OT texts like Isaiah 32:15; 44:3; Ezekiel 36:25-26 and Joel 2:28-29, are all prophecies concerning the giving of Spirit in the eschatological times. Thus, the Holy Spirit is the source of life and new life. The Spirit of the LORD can cleanse, restore, and renew all life including the victims of human trafficking and other crimes. It is the responsibility of the agents and facilitators to rescue the victims and give this assurance and enable the victims to make this conviction theirs and begin their life afresh.

Jesus Giver of Life and the Final Judge

Similarly, John 5:26 affirms that God the Father has life in himself, and has granted the Son Jesus to have life in himself. This is a reiteration of the truth stated earlier in John 1:4, "in him was life", which affirms the impartation of the life-in-himself in a timeless sense. Then in John 5:27, it is stated that God the Father has given to Jesus authority to execute judgment because he is the Son of Man. Theologically, John 5:26 affirms God as the source of life and depends on no one else for His/Her existence. The existence of God is conditioned by nothing and no one; life and the very being belong to the very nature of God the Father and the Son.[3] Therefore God is the "living Father" (John 6:57). St. Augustine made an insightful distinction between the 'life in himself' of the Son, and believers having eternal life. He asks, "Where does he [the Son] have it [life]? 'In himself.' Where has he [God] given it? 'In himself.' Where does Paul have? Not in himself, but in Christ. Where do you, a man of faith have it? Not in yourself, but in Christ."[4] Believers never have life in themselves but they have only and always mediated life.[5] This idea of common possession of life by the Father and the Son was interpreted as the *eternal*

3 K. Romaniuk, "'I am the Resurrection and the Life' (Jn 11:25)," *Concilium* 10/6 (1970), 70.

4 J. C. Elowsky, ed. *Ancient Christian Commentary on Scripture: New Testament*, IVA *John 1-10* (Illinois: IVP, 2006), 198, cited from Augustine, *Tractates on the Gospel of John.*

5 M. M. Thompson, "The Living Father," *Semia* 85 (1999), 26.

life of the Trinity in metaphysical sense, and used in the patristic argument against the Arianism (a thought which is a bit advanced than it might have been assumed by John).[6]

At any rate, the important point for us is that these verses provide us with theological grounds for the Son to give life and judge in the midst of forces of dead and life being trapped by death-dealing forces like human trafficking and its associated crimes.

The God of the Bible as the Creator, Author, and source of the life, thus, provides all good things for the sustenance and protection of life of all. More importantly, the God of Bible is the one who shows particular favour for the people who are most vulnerable to various evil designs of this world and become victims. We see that God not only created a world where all living beings co-exist and have fullness of life, but also prepared and prepares ways and means, and time and again intervened and intervenes into the affairs life through various mediators and facilitators to protect, liberate and rescue peoples, especially victims caught up in dangers, distress and crises. God also constantly inspires, calls, empowers and sends individuals, groups, and agencies to initiate, organize and participate in the process of prevention of human trafficking, slavery, and to do rescue and rehabilitation missions for victims caught in the tentacles of such crimes.

Despite the sanctity, beauty, and all good things of human life as designed by the Creator and redeemed in Jesus Christ, many in the ancient world and millions in the modern world became and continue to become victims of human trafficking and suffer all kinds of violence, stress, trauma and harassments. Let us look at some examples of such victims as well as the biblical faith resources for restoration and rehabilitation.

---

6 D. R. Sadananda, *The Johannine Exegesis of God: An Exploration into the Johannine Understanding of God* (Berlin/New York: Walter de Gruyter, 2004), 71.

Joseph as a Victim of Human Trafficking and a Model of Restoration

The story of Joseph is one of the most important biblical narratives which shed much light on human trafficking in the ancient Israel and in the Ancient Near East. It is fused with rich theological, moral and ethical ideas and issues informing us on the causes and effects of the crime of human trafficking. Many modern readers concerned with and involved in combating human trafficking, and restoration and rehabilitation of victims of human trafficking have turned to Joseph's experiences for inspiration and spiritual resources.[7]

The Root Causes

Many factors combine together to contribute to this crime of human trafficking.[8] We see ***a complex and complicated domestic violence*** in the form of partiality and favoritism of the parents, thereby hatred sown and shown among the members in the family in the Joseph's story, which are not always noted by commentators

7 E.g., see Roger Seth, "Joseph, Human Trafficking Survivor," in *Drishtikone: Evangelical Perspective on Mission and Ethics* 3 (2012), 8-11.

8 Anita Kanaiya, "Human Trafficking - A Modern Day Slavery?" in *Drishtikone: Evangelical Perspective on Mission and Ethics* 3 (2012): 3, rightly says that "it is not just poverty that causes vulnerability, but the combination of poverty, social exclusion and alienation, casteism, gender discrimination, lack of land, lack of access to or value of education, failure of agriculture to meet the needs of the local community throughout the year in rural trafficking hotspots, lack of alternatives to agricultural work in the locality, large-scale internal migration and although this is not negative in itself, it does lead to vulnerability to trafficking, not only in the process of seasonal migration, but also for children to grow up in the context where informal and ad hoc migration is considered the norm, increasing "merchandise character" of children within a globalised free market economy, high profit potential, growing tourism, growing national and international demand for child adoption, superstitious belief that sexual intercourse with very young girls (virgins) cures one from infectious diseases, natural catastrophes, war or economic depression increase the danger for children to become victims of child trafficking."

and writers.[9] Joseph also acted as a reporter of bad things of his brothers to the father (Gen 37:2). We see here how domestic violence in the form of pampering, partiality, favoritism, hatred, and animosity among siblings is transformed into a crime of human trafficking across international boundaries. Long before Joseph landed as a slave in the house of Potiphar in Egypt as a victim of human trafficking sold by his own brothers to the Ishmaelite traders, then falsely charged for adultery, and eventually landing up in a jail; the sins of enmity and hatred between the parents and children and between Joseph and his brothers were hatched at home unabated.

In this connection, it is appropriate to read the relevant text on the sins of favoritism in the family of Joseph's grandparents first, which says: "Isaac loved Esau, because he was fond of game; but Rebekah loved Jacob" (Gen 25:28).

The patriarch, Isaac, the father of Jacob died but the sin of his father showing exclusive favour to one of his children did not die in the family. Jacob also loved Joseph more than any of his children, because he was the son of his old age; and he had made him a long robe with sleeves (Gen 37:3). But, the story does not end there. Rather that is the beginning, the very root cause which contributed to hatred and enmity in the family that led to chain of domestic violence that stripped Joseph of his robe and dignity, throwing him into an empty pit and finally being sold to be a salve in a foreign country. This is supported by the passage which says:

> But, when his brothers saw that their father loved him [Joseph] more than all his brothers, ***they hated him, and could not speak peaceably to him*** (Gen 37:4).

As a result of these taken for granted favoritism, hatred, domestic violence and hurts, the brothers in the family were just waiting and looking for an opportunity to commit the crime. We see a clear connection between moral laxity and crime in a family

9 On domestic violence readers may refer *Voices against Domestic Violence: Biblical, Theological and Sociocultural Appraisal of the Experiences of the Oppressed Tribal, Children, Men and Women*, edited by A. Tali Ao (Mokokchung: CCPRA & Delhi: CWI, 2016).

sitting here. This is not to say that all crimes in the sight of law are sin. There are many accepted laws, customs, traditions and belief that abet and perpetrate acts of discriminations leading to crimes like human trafficking.

As such, although it was the brothers and the traders who actually committed the crime and should be awarded fitting punishment, the respected biblical patriarch, Jacob, should not get away but held as responsible for giving birth to the crime. The story and the texts clearly show that as we grapple with the multiple layers of crimes and larger dimensions of human trafficking involving myriad of pimps and agents of under dons we should not lost sight of the important factors which should be dealt with properly and timely to prevent such crime being developed within the confines of a family. We need homes in which true love combined with fair and justice is practiced and promoted. A home within which evil of favoritism is compromised and accepted consciously and unconsciously cannot fight against many evils out there in the society and culture. A healthy family relationship is an essential weapon to fight against many of the evils and crimes in the world today instead of waiting for the crimes to be committed and all hells broken at home and in the society.

The Victim Forgives and Reveals the Perpetrators' Cover-Ups for Healing

The rescue and rehabilitation of the victim in the story is further delayed and complicated. This is due to the cover-ups by the brothers of their crime. First they lied to their father. This is what the text says:

> Then they [Joseph's brothers] took Joseph's robe, slaughtered a goat, and dipped the robe in the blood. They had the long robe with sleeves taken to their father, and they said, "This we have found; see now whether it is *your* son's robe or not" (Gen 37:31-32).

Secondly, they lied to their brother Joseph. When they went to Egypt to buy grains they tried to conceal their wrong doings and said, "We are honest men". This expression is repeated like a refrain in the narrative (Gen 42:11, 19, 31, 33, 34).

In spite of their realization, they did not open up to their brother because of fear of retaliation (Gen 50:15). And this led them to more repressed guilt feelings and the toxic emotions remained unhealed in them. This is reflected in their words, "Alas, we are paying the penalty for what we did to our brother; we saw his anguish when he pleaded with us, but we would not listen. That is why this anguish has come upon us" (Gen 42:21). It is in such situation the biblical injunction clearly states the need to ***confess*** and ***turn away*** from evil doings for healing. It says, "No one who conceals transgression will prosper, but one who confesses and forsakes them will obtain mercy" (Proverbs 28:13).

Joseph's brothers and family members were reconciled and reunited with Joseph because he as ***the victim accepted the perpetrators of the crime he suffered and forgave them of their wrong doings***. Joseph saw in his ordeals and in the wicked designs of his brothers God's plan to preserve life and a remnant on earth amid natural and human made calamities. He says:

> And now do not be distressed, or angry with yourselves, because you sold me here; for God sent me before you to preserve life. For the famine has been in the land these two years; and there are five more years in which there will be neither plowing nor harvest. God sent me before you to preserve for you a remnant on earth, and to keep alive for you many survivors. So it was not you who sent me here, but God; he has made me a father to Pharaoh and lord of all his house and ruler over all the land of Egypt.... Even though you intended to do harm to me, God intended it for good, in order to preserve a numerous people, as he is doing today. So have no fear; I myself will provide for you and your little ones." In this way he reassured them, speaking kindly to them. (Gen 45:5-8; 50:19-21).

Unlike the commonly and generally accepted norm and practice of the perpetrators seeking forgiveness and paying all compensations for damage, lost, and injury and injustice done to the victims, the Joseph story shows and ends the other way around. It is *the victim* who accepts, forgives, gives full assurance and pays in full everything and much more for the reconciliation, reunion, and healing of all parties involved. In this regard, Julie Waters cogently comments:

> Forgiveness is understandably a sensitive topic for victims of crime. The narrative of Joseph closes with Joseph fully forgiving his brothers.... When Jacob, their father, dies, the brothers are concerned that Joseph will now exact revenge upon them. Instead of enacting revenge, Joseph reassures of them of his forgiveness and continued provision for them and their families.... In no way should human trafficking victims ever be forced to forgive their traffickers, but forgiveness does play a role in the healing process. Forgiveness is not an easy process, and it takes times. Harboring anger and resentment towards the trafficker allows the trafficker to continue to exert an influence over a victim that has been physically freed from captivity. Forgiveness does not diminish the offense that occurred nor does it lessen the accountability of the offender. Instead, forgiveness frees the victim from anger, fear and bitterness and sets the victim free from the power of the trafficker.[10]

Joseph as a victim forgiving the criminals of their wrong doings and opening the ways for reconciliation and healing, he foreshadows the model of Jesus who as a victim of injustice forgave and forgives all who sinned and committed crimes against him and continue to sin and commit crimes thereby bringing reconciliation, healing and wholeness.

Biblical Legislation Relating to Human Trafficking

There are also other ways of dealing with the crime of human trafficking in the Bible. This may be called the legal or legislation model to address the issue. The model as represented by Joseph's story and insights therein for understanding and handling issues

---

10 Julie Waters, "The Intersection of Law, Theology, and Human Trafficking in The Narrative of Joseph: Linking the Past to the Present," in *Second Annual Interdisciplinary Conference on Human Trafficking,* 2010. 8, http://digitalcommons.unl.edu/humtrafconf2/8. Accessed on 16/11/2017.

related to criminal activities involved in human trafficking and the need for healing of the victims and the perpetrators may be helpful in some cases. But, certainly there may be other cases and situations where the law of the land may have to take its own course to bring justice, healing and arrived at a sense of closure for the victims who undergo protracted trauma and post-traumatic stress disorder. Sometimes a combination of both these ways or models and many more other ways and means may be required to address the concerns of rescue, rehabilitation, and healing.

In this regard, it is very heartening to know that the Bible also deals with human trafficking very seriously and firmly. It is treated as a capital crime and the offender is awarded a capital punishment by death. The Bible gives unambiguous theological and ethical injunctions against human trafficking. This is unlike several other social problems we face today, problems which often leave us with controversial and divided stands and we are unable to reach a biblically and/or a religiously solid ground but only a divided opinion making us more vulnerable to violence, discrimination, injustice, and crimes. Let us look at some biblical passages that categorically prohibit human trafficking in any form.

Exodus 21:16

Exodus 20:22-23:19 is commonly known as 'the covenant code' or 'the book of the covenant' as referred to in Exodus 24:27.[11] Within this larger section, Exodus 21:12-17 deal with capital offences and Exodus 21:18-32 with noncapital crimes. Exodus chapter twenty one verses 12-17 mention five instances, namely: striking a person mortally, willfully attacking and killing by treachery, striking father or mother, kidnapping a person, cursing father or

---

11 Walter Brueggemann, "The Book of Exodus: Introduction, Commentary, and Reflections," in Leander E. Keck, et al., eds., *The New Interpreter's Bible: General Articles & Introduction, Commentary, & Reflections for Each Book of the Bible Including the Apocryphal/Deuterocanonical Books in Twelve Volumes*, vol. I (Nashville: Abingdon Press, 1994), 855; See also John F. Craghan, "Exodus," in William R. Farmer, et al., eds., *The International Bible Commentary: An Ecumenical Commentary for the Twenty-First Century* (Bangalore: TPI, 1998, 2004), 482.

mother, all of these offences will be punished by death penalty. The whole section is concerned with the sanctity and dignity of individual persons and the safety and security of his/her life. The relevant text for our purpose is 21:16: It says:

> Whoever kidnaps a person, whether that person has been sold or is still held in possession, shall be put to death.

Here is an explicit law against human-stealing in the Bible. In this regard, a Japanese commentator says, "Kidnapping is the most extreme form of theft. As such the kidnapper shall be put to death."[12] The Hebrew word *genub*, means to steal or rob, i.e., *he that steals a man* which is translated as *klepse,* i.e., to steal (a person, man, woman, or child), in the LXX, with design to sell him/her to the Gentiles (for no Israelite would buy him/her), was adjudged to death by this statute, which is ratified by the apostle Paul in 1 Timothy 1:10, where *human-stealers* are reckoned among those wicked ones against whom stringent laws must be made by states.[13]

Another commentator on Exodus 21:16, says, "Manstealing and kidnapping, as well as the sale into slavery of those abducted, were capital offences. This was also true in the ancient Babylonian code which, however, concentrates on kidnapping (Code of Hammurabi 14). Deuteronomy 24:7 specifies that this penalty applies to the abduction of Israelites."[14]

Deuteronomy 24:7

This is another text on law against man-stealing. It was not death by the law of Moses to steal cattle or goods; but to steal a child,

---

12 Yuichi Osumi, "Deuteronomy," in William R. Farmer, et al., eds., *The International Bible Commentary: An Ecumenical Commentary for the Twenty-First Century* (Bangalore: TPI, 1998, 2004), 564.

13 Matthew Henry's note on Exodus 21:16. The citations of Matthew Henry's notes are from the electronic version of his commentary in the *Bible Works 7* as such no bibliographical data are furnished.

14 J. Coert Rylaarsdam, "The Book of Exodus: Introduction and Exegesis," in *The Interpreter's Bible*, vol. I, ed. G. Arthur Buttrick (New York: Abingdon, 1952), 998.

or a weak and simple person, or one that a man had in his power, and to make merchandize of him, this was a capital crime, and could not be expiated, as other thefts, by restitution so much is *a human better than a sheep* (Matthew 12:12). It was a very heinous offence on three counts. ***First,*** it was robbing the public of one of its members. ***Secondly***, it was taking away a person's liberty, the liberty of a free-born Israelite, which was next in value to his life. ***Thirdly***, it was driving a person out from the inheritance of the land, to the privileges of which s/he was entitled, and bidding her/him go serve other gods, as David complains against Saul when the latter hunted him and made him fugitive (1 Samuel 26:19).[15]

Besides kidnapping and human trafficking, there are some other offences like the theft of property belonging to God, i.e., the devoted things (*herem)* which were punished by death like in the case of Achan (Joshua 7:1, 18-25).

Before we move further two comments are in order. First, for those who in some way may think that these laws are overly legal and perhaps legalistic and hence dry, they must remember the high respect accorded to the values of life in the Bible as God's gift which must be guarded at any cost when endangered or robbed of its dignity and quality by sin or/and crime. Hence, the laws convey Israel's regard for human persons' life, a value that stands out when viewed against other Ancient Near Eastern legal codes.[16] And in the context of the quantum of crimes committed deliberately against human life due to greed and selfish motives, states and global community need to rethink the insights and helpfulness of relevant laws and strengthen their grips and implement them to check and combat crimes that threaten and destroy life.

Second, the law prohibiting kidnapping differently worded in the two texts is essentially the same. In a tribal community, members of an alien tribe especially children readily became targets of abuse and illicit use, more so in times of conflicts

15 Matthew Henry's note on Deut 24:7 in the *Bible Works 7*.

16 John F. Craghan, "Exodus," in William R. Farmer, et al., eds. *The International Bible Commentary: An Ecumenical Commentary for the Twenty-First Century* (Bangalore: TPI, 1998, 2004), 482.

and wars. The law applying only to Israelites is quite disturbing and weakens the basic principle of protection of human life and dignity of all. This reflects the election and covenant theology and ideology that permeate the OT which extend privileges to Israelites to the exclusion of others. Such exclusions were challenged by the later prophets (Jonah and Ruth protest the exclusivistic and isolationistic religious ideology).[17] Jesus removed all barriers in the sharing of God's love and grace (John 4:7-15; Galatians 3:28-29, if you belong to Christ, then you are Abraham's offspring, heirs according o the promise').

Prophets Protested against All Forms of Slavery and Exploitations

One of the most controversial subjects relating to human trafficking is the slavery which has direct bearing on human life, dignity and human rights. Slavery as part of socioeconomic support system permeated human society in all times and places in various forms.[18] The three types of slavery in Israel were: slaves by birth, slaves by purchase, and people captured in war turned to slaves. Various laws relating to slavery could not adequately rise up to the expectations of the high values and ideals enshrined in the covenant enacted as a result of God's deliverance and liberation of Israel from Egyptian slavery (Deuteronomy 15:15; cf. Leviticus 25:42-45). As a result prophets protested and criticized slavery practices and called Israel to 'break every yoke' and 'let the oppressed go free' (2 Chronicles 28:8-15; Isaiah 58:6). In particular Jeremiah denounced slavery and announced God's judgment against continued holding and ill treatment of slaves against God's will. He says:

17 Daniel Jones Muthunayagom, "Election in Relation to Mission of the Church in a Religiously Pluralistic Context: An Old Testament Perspective," *Bangalore Theological Forum* XLI/1 (June 2009), 109.

18 Willard M. Swartley, "Slavery," in Joel B. Green, et al. eds. *Dictionary of Scripture and Ethics* (Grand Rapids, Michigan: Backer Academic, 2011), 736.

> Thus says the LORD, the God of Israel: I myself made a covenant with your ancestors when I brought them out of the land of Egypt, out of the house of slavery, saying, "Every seventh year each of you must set free any Hebrews who have been sold to you and have served you six years; you must set them free from your service." But, your ancestors did not listen to me or incline their ears to me. You yourselves recently repented and did what was right in my sight by proclaiming liberty to one another, and you made a covenant before me in the house that is called by my name; but then you turned around and profaned my name when each of you took back your male and female slaves, whom you had set free according to their desire, and you brought them again into subjection to be your slaves. Therefore, thus says the LORD: You have not obeyed me by granting a release to your neighbors and friends; I am going to grant a release to you, says the LORD-a release to the sword, to pestilence, and to famine. I will make you a horror to all the kingdoms of the earth. And those who transgressed my covenant and did not keep the terms of the covenant that they made before me… shall be handed over to their enemies and to those who seek their lives. Their corpses shall become food for the birds of the air and the wild animals of the earth. And as for King Zedekiah of Judah and his officials, I will hand them over to their enemies and to those who seek their lives, to the army of the king of Babylon, which has withdrawn from you. I am going to command says the LORD, and will bring them back to this city; and they will fight against it, and take it, and burn it with fire. The towns of Judah I will make a desolation without inhabitant (Jeremiah 34:13-22).

Prophets also looked to the days when God's Spirit will be poured on all including the male and female slaves with a view to enjoy full freedom of life in all dimensions (Joel 2:29, cf. Acts 2:18). 'Now the Lord is the Spirit, and where the Spirit of the Lord is, there is freedom' (2 Corinthians 3:17).

Jesus' Programmatic and Paradigmatic Proclamation of Freedom and Liberty for All

Against the backdrop of all kinds of exploitations of people by the Roman rulers and authorities irrespective of nationalities, race, gender, class, and similar evil practices among the Jews, Jesus announced his mission and ministry as the release of all the oppressed. Luke narrates and locates this moment strategically and programmatically at beginning of Jesus' public ministry in Nazareth probably on a Jewish Jubilee celebration day. He writes:

> When he came to Nazareth, where he had been brought up, he went to the synagogue on the Sabbath day, as was his custom. He stood up to read, and the scroll of the prophet Isaiah was given to him. He unrolled the scroll and found the place where it was written:
>
> The Spirit of the Lord is upon me,
> Because he has anointed me to bring good news to the poor.
> He has sent me to proclaim release to the captives.
> And recovery of sight to the blind,
> To let the oppressed go free,
> To proclaim the year of the Lord's favour.
>
> And he rolled up the scroll, gave it back to the attendant, and sat down. The eyes of all in the synagogue were fixed on him. Then he began to say to them, "Today this scripture has been fulfilled in your hearing" (Luke 4:16-21).

Jesus goes beyond the OT legislations and laws, and turned conventional cultures and customs on their heads and set unprecedented standards of righteousness and justice to be measured by the values, models and examples embodied in his life as the incarnation of God and His/Her will and rule on earth. He challenged the crowd saying, "Unless your righteousness exceeds that of the scribes and Pharisees, you will never enter the kingdom of heaven" (Matthew 5:20). In order to break down all forced servitude, slavery, forced labour, and dismantle all forms of exploitation, oppression, commodification and capitalization, classification of human beings made in the image of God, he took the form of slave in him (Philippians 2:7). He declared that as the Son of Man he 'came not to be served but to serve, and to give his life a ransom for many' (Mark 10:45).

Risking his life he protested in the Jerusalem Temple in public which was the heart of Jewish religious, sociopolitical, and illicit commercial hub (Mark 11:15-19; Mt 21:12-17; Luke 19:45-48; John 2:13-22). He boldly challenged and razed down its illicit daily business transactions.[19] Symbolically, he replaced it with his risen body. He demanded that henceforth true worshipers need not get entangled with inadequate if not barren religiously sanctioned spaces and rites but simply go to the Father in spirit and truth to worship Him/Her and get nurtured their life gifted by God and redeemed by his precious blood and sustained by the Holy Spirit who is the advocate of the victims of human made religious trappings, evils, and crimes of the world (John 3:14; 4:23; 14:15-17; 15:26-27).

It was some of the religious and political leaders associated with the official Judaism centered in the temple whom Jesus called "the thief" who comes only to steal and kill and destroy. It is against such people with whom Jesus confronted in his ministry and contrasted his mission as to give life, and give it abundantly (John 10:10). Jesus' use of the word 'thief', *kleptes* in Greek recalls the *klepse,* i.e., to steal in Exodus 21:16 and Deuteronomy 24:7 which we saw in the OT laws relating to human-stealing or human trafficking. This in some way shows that Jesus in his ministry was combating some form of human trafficking and illicit trading of other resources meant for the support of life of those belonging to the weaker sections. Due to the vested interest of the leaders and responsible people entrusted to guide, lead, and take care of the people; many both Jews and non-Jews were caught in all kinds of evil designs of the society. They were like the sheep without shepherd. When Jesus "saw the crowds, he had compassion for

19 S. P. Mathew, *Temple-Criticism in Mark's Gospel: the Economic Role of the Jerusalem Temple during the First Century CE* (Delhi: ISPCK, 1999), 72-75.

them, because they were harassed and helpless, like sheep without a shepherd" (Matthew 9:36).

Jesus' response to such situation, evils, harassment, exploitation, oppression in any form either by human agents, establishments, institutionalized or organized crimes, possession by evil spirit, sicknesses and diseases, etc., involved invoking the power of God and the working of the Holy Spirit along with the recognition of faith of the victims and sufferers and their quest for healing and healthy life.

At the same time, frequently he referred to the word of God in the scriptures and prayed to God for healing, rescue, rising from dead, and rehabilitation. All these expressions came out of his compassion on the victims and his passion to do the work and will of God which is to bring God's salvation and to give fullness of life and to get involved in doing the salvific work of God, i.e., good works in the world ('to do good', Mark 3:4). All these activities of Jesus were part and extension of his proclamation and demonstration of the coming of the kingdom or reign, or rule of God on earth. The key to receive the liberation, salvation and redemption that God is offering to the world in and through Jesus is to repent and believe in the good news as embodied in Jesus' life and work. Again and again Jesus said to the sick and paralyzed people, "your sins are forgiven", as part of healing and setting people free or release them from various bondages (Matthew 9:2; Luke 7:48).

Paul and Slavery

There is no space and time to go into all the intricate debate surrounding this problem in Pauline writings. But, just to clear the air of doubt on Paul's attitude toward slavery in his time, let me just state some basic points which may help us for further discussion. Slavery functions as a metaphor of Christian life in Paul's writings. In view of the multivalent meanings of slavery in the Roman society, Paul uses 'slave of Christ' (Romans 1:1; Galatians1:10; Philippians1:1), to enhance his status and authority or 'slave of all' (1 Cor 9:19) to lower himself to identify with slaves. It is also used to designate divine ownership and devotion to Christ or/and God as Lord. Assuming the immediate inability to do away with slavery all of a sudden, New Testament letters give certain exhortations to regulate the conduct of salves and masters as belonging to the body of Christ. They reflect the slaves' significant standing in the Christian community (Ephesians 6:5-9; Colossians 3:22-4:1; 1Timothy 6:1-2; Titus 2:9-10; 1 Peter 2:18-19). They affirm that Jesus' liberating gospel abolishes status distinction between slaves and free in the Christian community (1 Corinthians 12:13; Galatians 3:28; Colossians 3:11). Slaves and masters alike are accountable to the Lord, thus jettisoning social and temporal slavery by the reality of new creation, in which all believers are slaves of Christ.

Paul's letter to Philemon also transforms slavery. Paul instructs Philemon to receive his runaway slave Onesimus back as a brother 'both in flesh and in the Lord' in the same way he would receive Paul himself (Philemon 16f.). Affirming the equality of slave and the free, the Christian gospel subverts the slavery generally accepted in the Greco-Roman society.[20]

By way of Conclusion

The bottom line is that human trafficking, slavery in any form, illicit commercialization, capitalization of human beings and their organs, and the like sharply contradict the content, message and principles of the gospel, the good news of God which Jesus came to proclaim, embody, live, was crucified, and raised from the dead. As such there is no ground for any form of slavery, pro-slavery stance and promoting any seemingly charity network to support the so called helpless children and child labour at home, in work places, factories or anywhere.

The model and paradigm of Jesus and the apostles to combat human trafficking, slavery, and child labour is the model of servanthood. Jesus became a slave to serve the oppressed that are

---

20 The views of this section are mainly from Willard M. Swartley, "Slavery," 736. For fuller discussion and debate on the different positions of scholars on the issue of slavery readers may refer to Willard M. Swartley, *Slavery, Sabbath, War and Women: Case Issues in Biblical Interpretation* (Scottdale, Pennsylvania: Herald Press, 1983), 31-64.

in need and subvert the oppressors, the tyrants, and the lords. Paul and other apostles give similar expression in their writing. If all disciples of Jesus today take up this model at home, at working places, in society, in public places, etc., that will challenge and revolutionize the easing going and lazy societal mindset and system that promotes lazy people, pleasure loving persons, and will reduce if not stop totally human trafficking in any form.

7

Human Trafficking in North East India
A Theological Response

Lovely Awomi James

Introduction

Nothing disturbs and agonizes us more than the horrific stories of modern day slavery namely human trafficking. The horrors of domestic, sexual and labour violence that trafficked-victims continue to suffer and endure in the hands of their traders and handlers, defy the scope of our imaginations. To realize and acknowledge that such thing is happening in our own neighbourhoods, towns and in our own region, is unbelievable yet it is happening and has been for quite long. The truth of the matter is that, we can no longer feign ignorance or remain in the most comfortable state of denial. Real situations compel us, now, to address the evil of human trafficking in our region. As the title suggests, this paper will briefly reflect upon the menace of human trafficking in North East India and attempt to give a theological response, from a tribal Christian perspective. Be cautioned however that the present writer's main objective is to provoke the participants and readers for critical theological discourse on the subject rather than presuming to give any absolute or universal theological response to the issue under discussion.

1. Human Trafficking: Modern Day Slave Trade

Human trafficking as modern day slave trade has shifted the history of slavery to its most monstrous form. We had believed and want to continue to do so, that slavery is no more in our present civilized world; that the world communities no longer condone or promote it; that it was abolished once and for all. However, the reality of human trafficking belies and ridicules any such claims. On the contrary, slavery has taken a completely new and worse turn – thriving illegally with millions of victims literally imprisoned and murdered without any hope and without any way out.

According to the definition given by the United Nations, human trafficking is,

> ... the recruitment, transportation, transfer, harbouring or receipt of persons, by means of the threat or use of force or other forms of coercion, of abduction, of fraud, of deception, of the abuse of power or of a position of vulnerability or of the giving or receiving of payments or benefits to achieve the consent of a person having control over another person, for the purpose of exploitation. Exploitation shall include, at a minimum, the exploitation of the prostitution of others or other forms of sexual exploitation, forced labour or services, slavery or practices similar to slavery, servitude or the removal of organs.[1]

As such human trafficking can simply be understood as a process in which persons – men, women and children, are transported from their homes, neighbourhoods, communities and countries to a certain destination for purpose of exploitation. Their exploitation include forced labour, prostitution, entertainment, industry, beggary, illegal adoption of children, forced marriage, drug trafficking, camel jockeys,[2] organs harvesting and murder;

---

1 "On Human Trafficking: A Biblical Perspective," in *https://www.unodc.org/documents/treaties/UNTOC/Publications/TOC%20* Convention/TOCebook-e.pdf (Accessed 7th November 2017).

2 Nishant Anand, *Women in India: The Problem of Missing Girl Child* (New Delhi: New Century Publications, 2016), 47.

besides others. Human trafficking stands as the third most profitable illegal trafficking industry after arms and drugs in the world. It is estimated that annually 27 [to 30] million people are falling victim to human trafficking at the global scale.[3] Trafficking takes place either by tricking the parents and guardians of the victims or by direct kidnapping and abductions. Victims are lured into different forms of slavery with the promise of good jobs, schooling and education. Sometimes, young girls are tricked into the romantic bliss of marriage and then sold off to brothels in the cities. Human trafficking is brought about not only through micro reasons of personal/community material and economic poverty but it also has macro reasons – at national and international level.

Owing to the so-called economic globalization – the new global economic order wherein there is the internationalization of trade and finance[4] which further gives birth to market globalism and renders the poor and developing countries dependent upon the rich countries. The poor countries often find themselves either struggling for the survival of their countries or, struggling to pay off their debts to the rich countries. Such situations lure the poor nations to engage in inhuman and illegal trades including human trafficking. Besides, we should also realize that there are two key elements of globalization that cater to the traffickers: improved communications and international trading networks.[5] Today, the information technologies are making it very easy for the traffickers to strike deals and arrange movement of trafficked victims without being caught.

---

3 Kathryn Farr, *Sex Trafficking: The Global Market in Women and Children* (New York: Worth Publishers, 2005), 25.

4 T. Swami Raju, *Christian Theological Response: Contemporary Contextual Concerns* (New Delhi: CWI, 2014), 139.

5 Jayant Choudhury and Manoshi Das, "Combating Human Trafficking with the NGOs in North-Eastern States: Some Suggestive Roles," in Awadhesh Kumar Singh, Atul Pratap Singh and Parvez Ahmed Khan, eds., *Trafficking in Women and Children in India: Emerging Perspectives, Issues and Strategies* (New Delhi: Serials Publications, 2012), 494. (Hereafter cited as Choudhury and Das, "Combating Human Trafficking with the NGOs in North-Eastern States...").

Trafficked victims go through the worst kind of slavery in our world today. They often find themselves imprisoned either by physical restraint or by intimidation from their captors and handlers. They find themselves without any ray of hope as their very own existence as real and living persons come under threat due to the seizure or confiscation of their legal proofs (documents) of their existence and citizenship by their captors.[6] This renders the victims to refrain from trying to escape and seek help as they have nothing on them to proof their citizenship and also they fear for further legal repercussions on themselves due to their state. Though there has been a call for national and international standards to protect the victims of human trafficking from being prosecuted as criminals yet that alone will not suffice. The nations of the world ought to seriously work on the legislations to help destroy the systems that protect and promote human trafficking.

2. Human Trafficking in North East India: The Reality

The North Eastern region is home to more than 200 tribal groups and it is socially and culturally distinct from the mainstream India. The region is surrounded by as many as four international borders and is connected to the mainland India only by a narrow corridor along the Assam-Bengal border. Such geographical positioning of the region makes it highly vulnerable to many illegal trans-border movements and activities like militants, arms, drugs and human trafficking. Bangladesh and Myanmar borders are considered to be the most affected international borders with illegal activities.[7] A study across eight states reveals that they are rich in resources but very poor in infrastructure and conflict-ridden. In addition to that, it also reveals that there is a huge rising in human trafficking and mostly women and children.[8] The nature of human trafficking

---

6 "Remember our Slavery: Jesus and Human Trafficking," in *http://www.scrib.com* (Accessed 8th November 2017).

7 "Fight Against Child Trafficking: Challenges before the Media," in *https://www.unodc.org/pdf/india/shillong.../Fight_Against_Child_Trafficking.pdf* (Accessed 10th November 2017).

8 Choudhury and Das, "Combating Human Trafficking with the NGOs in North-Eastern States...", 499.

in the region is two-fold: trafficking-in of persons from other countries like Nepal, Myanmar and Bangladesh; and, trafficking-out of persons from the region to other metropolitan cities, regions and outside the country. Most of those trafficked-in from other neighbouring states and countries are engaged in cheap labour, in coal mines in Meghalaya, in tea gardens in Assam and in prostitution.[9]

According to the survey report on the NEI states, Assam tops the list in human trafficking with the highest number of human trafficking cases in the country in 2015.[10] It accounts for 22% of the total reported cases of trafficking across India. Besides, it also has the highest number of child trafficking cases (1,317), which makes up 33% of the national figure.[11] This, points to a serious violation of child rights in our region. Assam is followed by Meghalaya, Tripura, Nagaland, Arunachal Pradesh, Manipur, Mizoram and Sikkim. As such, the chairperson of Assam State Commission for Protection of Child Rights, Runumi Gogoi stated that it (Assam) has become a major source area for human trafficking to the rest of the country. She further identifies that most of the trafficking takes place in the tea garden areas and that widespread poverty and illiteracy among the tea gardeners are prime factors for human trafficking among them. Illiteracy rate among the tea workers is

---

9 A Nedan Foundation study report. Ibid.

10 Union Minister of State for Home, Hansraj Gangaram Ahir states, "According to information collected and compiled by the National Crime Records Bureau from all the states and Union territories in 2015, 6,877 cases of human trafficking were reported. Of this, 1,539 cases were reported from the Northeastern States." Out of these 1,539 cases, 1,494 cases were registered from Assam. Cf. "Assam Tops Human Trafficking List," The Telegraph (Thursday, November 9, 2017, in *https://www.google.co.in/search?dcr=0&source=hp&ei=RdoDWvulcTmvgTuiKsw&q=human+trafficking+in+north+east+india&oq=Human+Trafficking+in+North+&gs_i=psy-ab.1.0.0l10.1870.13237.0.15610.29.27.1.0.0.0.319.3919.0j19j2j1.22.0....0...1.1.64.psy-ab..6.23.3937...0i131k1j0i10k1.0NBe-FrHxu1M* (Accessed 9th November 2017).

11 "Child Rights Violations and Trafficking Haunting North-East India," in *https://reliefweb.int/report/india/child-rights-violations-and-trafficking-haunting-north-east-india* (Accessed 9th Novenber 2017).

as high as 75 percent and hence traffickers take advantage of their lack of education and economic backwardness for their illegal businesses. Despite the state government's attempt to implement the Right to Education Act (RTE) 2009 and the Plantation Labour Act in the tea garden areas for the improvement of the living conditions of the workers, the rate of trafficked victims is on the increase.

Tea garden communities are not the only ones vulnerable to human trafficking. People and communities affected by ethnic violence, natural calamities, unemployment, distressed migration, economic poverty and so forth are also equally vulnerable to trafficking as they become easy preys to those traders and handlers of human trafficking. It is also reported that since 2012, 4,754 children in Assam have gone missing, of whom 2,753 are girls.[12] The region is also a hotspot for ethnic conflicts as people of diverse ethnicity live together or in close proximity to each other. Take for instance the Bodo and Adivasi conflict in Bodo Land Territorial Autonomous District Council (BTAD) since 1996 where the victims have been living till date in the camps without any proper shelter, sanitation and health facilities, livelihood and education for children. There are numerous cases of women and young girls being trafficked from those camps for purpose of domestic work in different parts of the country and outside like Bhutan and Nepal.[13] It is said that traffickers find a safe haven for child labour in Bhutan where many of the trafficked children are put to work under different harmful environment.

2.1. Factors Responsible for Rendering People Vulnerable to Human Trafficking in the Region

Following are some of the factors that lure the vulnerable victims to human traffickers in the region:

---

12 Ibid.

13 Elizabeth Devi, Prateeti Barman, "Women in Conflict Situations and Human Rights Violations: Experiences from Northeast India," in Daisy Bora Talukdar, ed., *Gender, Peace and Development in North East India* (Guwahati: DVS Publishers, 2012), 123.

1. Economic Poverty – want of food and basic human necessities.
2. Lack of development in the region – want of better standard of life and facilities.
3. Lack of job opportunities for both the educated and the uneducated.
4. Craze for global cultural lifestyle – many of the region's youngsters become victims when recruiters come to them with promises of their lives' dreams. There is a huge loss of cultural identity.
5. Decline in tribal cultural values – e.g., work culture and the dignity of labour.
6. Failure in imbibing Christian moral-ethical teachings
7. Traditional attitude toward what is acceptable profession/job and what is not.
8. Lack of information and awareness of human trafficking among the masses.
9. Parental negligence of children either due to illiteracy or sheer ignorance.

3. Human Trafficking in North East India: A Theological Response

Attempting to give a theological response to the problem of human trafficking in the region is not as easy as it sounds or as one thinks it to be. Therefore, here is a humble attempt as the writer approaches the subject with honest fear and trepidation.

3.1. What Does the Bible Say about Human Trafficking?

Before we proceed with any semblance of a theological response, it is imperative that we briefly attempt to understand what the Bible has to say in regard to human trafficking – a sinful act of harming and enslaving the vulnerable. Slavery was neither new nor non-existent both during the Old and the New Testament periods. It flourished in different forms and norms, for example, bonded slavery as a result of debt, enslaving of a race (the Hebrews in Egypt), socio-cultural sanction of owning slaves for household labour, slave trade and so on. Few biblical insights are therefore highlighted here for our deliberation and discourse.

3.1.1. God Sides with the Victims

One familiar story of human trafficking that we read in the Bible is that of Joseph in Genesis 37. Joseph, the youngest son of Jacob and Rachel, was sold off to the Ishmaelites by his half-brothers for twenty pieces of silver. The end result of the story reveals that God was on the side of the victim, protecting and using him (Joseph) for the blessing of both Egypt (where he was taken to) and the descendants of Israel including his traders (brothers). Besides, Joseph also confronted his brothers with their crime (Genesis 50:20), to let them know that what they did to him was a crime, wrong and that God was on his side. This story can be a huge source of comfort and hope for the victims of human trafficking; knowing and experiencing the love, blessings and protection of the all-seeing God on their side.

3.1.2. Death Penalty for Slave Traders and Traffickers According to the Law

In Deuteronomy 24:7 says:

> If someone is caught kidnapping another Israelite, enslaving or selling the Israelite, then that kidnapper shall die. So you shall purge the evil from your midst. [NRSV]

It strongly sanctions death penalty for the kidnapper, abductor and trader. While the law here speaks of an Israelite harming another Israelite, it applies to any and every person irrespective of tribe, nationality, sex, colour and creed that any form of human trafficking is an abomination to the Lord and that it is punishable by law. Today we have international, national and regional laws and legislations that documents clearly on the consequences of human trafficking and exploitation of all kinds and yet, they remain mostly in papers and in the offices of the lawmakers. The laws of the nations state that slave traders, exploiters and traffickers are punishable under the law but the systems and those responsible for executing the law either neglect or are accomplices in one form or the other of the criminals. This victimizes the victims doubly and they do not get any justice in their lives.

3.1.3. The Bible Condemns Human Trafficking (Slave Trade)

The New Testament specifically condemns human trafficking or slave trade along with other crimes such as murder, lying, sodomy, fornication and so on. 1Timothy 1:8-11 reads:

> Now we know that the law is good, if one uses it legitimately. This means...the law is laid down not for the innocent but for the lawless and disobedient, for the godless and sinful, for the unholy and profane, for those who kill their father or mother, for murderers, fornicators, sodomites, **slave traders** [emphasis added], liars, perjurers, and whatever else is contrary to the sound teaching that conforms to the glorious gospel of the blessed God, which he entrusted to me. [NRSV].

We too must condemn human trafficking. With the scriptures, as mentioned, we also have laws that spell out human trafficking, traffickers, slave traders and the like to be condemned by one and all and render fitting punishment to them. Until and unless each of us as rightful citizens of a nation and state take our right to action against this human trafficking, the laws will continue to remain in sheets of papers only.

3.1.4. The Bible Entreats the Release of One's Slaves

We read of Paul entreating his brother and friend-in-the-Lord, Philemon, to release the latter's slave Onesimus from their former relationship of master and slave. Paul pleads (rather than commands) with Philemon to review his relationship with his former slave and to receive him anew as a beloved brother rather than as his slave. He also makes sure that Philemon understands that he (Paul) does not want him to feel pressured or forced to release his slave but instead he must do this on his own good volition which is grounded upon the Gospel of Christ. This clearly tells us that slavery has no place in our faith in Christ. As long as we condone, practice and promote slavery of any kind, we are not true followers of Christ. Slavery of any kind is robbing someone of his/her freedom and human right and hence, it contradicts with our faith and the Good News of our Lord Jesus Christ. Tribal homes/families still have the shadow of slavery in the guise of helpers/servants in our households. While many of our helpers might not be the direct victims of human trafficking, they are nevertheless either smuggled victims, tricked or even simply victims of family poverty whereby they end up being enslaved in their work places and homes. In much of the tribal Christian homes, we find them being overworked, discriminated and abused either or both verbally and physically. If that is not enslavement what is it? We need to ponder upon this also.

3.1.5. Jesus, the Liberator, the Good News for the Enslaved

Jesus' famous Nazareth Manifesto in Luke 4:10-19 reads:

> The Spirit of God is upon me, because he has anointed me to bring good news to the poor. He has sent me to proclaim release to the captives and recovery of sight to the blind, to let the oppressed go free, to proclaim the year of the Lord's favour. [NRSV]

While we can draw several implications from this passage, let us be contended here with one of its stark messages – that Jesus is the bringer of God's Good News to all those who are enslaved under different forms of slavery and oppression. He is the Good News, the Hope and the Liberator for the victims of human trafficking and its varied evils. As North East region is afflicted with the widespread disease of human trafficking especially of women and young boys and girls, let us find hope and give hope to the victims of God's power of love, healing and salvation in their lives. Jesus' earthly ministry is filled with his immeasurable compassion toward the outcasts and the oppressed: the poor, women, boys and girls of his time. Are we also ready to follow his steps and his example as his true followers?

3.2. A Theological Anthropology based on the Imago Dei is Necessary

A theological anthropology needs a revisiting. Human life as sacred and as the image of God needs to be re-affirmed and re-established. The Bible tells us that in the beginning God created the humans – male and female in God's own likeness. This stamp of the divine should be re-affirmed and acknowledged in human life so as to orient people and individuals to value, respect and protect lives. We need to re-interpret the doctrine of the image of God in the context where humans have lost their wisdom and their reasoning power to understand that life is grounded in God; that it is God who created and gave us life; that we are accountable to God and that we are to love, nurture and save lives rather than devalue, disrespect and destroy or take lives.

We need to re-define the meaning of God's image in humans. Theologians have, for centuries attempted to connect the image of God with different views: for instance, functional view – with subduing and ruling; substantive or structural view – with the identification of rationality or reason in the soul; relational or social view – with social, interpersonal relations between peoples and communities. The first connects the image of God with dominion and ruling; the second with the soul's capacity to reason and carry out the function of care and or subduing the earth; the third connects the image with the relational idea of God-as given in Genesis 1:26 "Let us make humankind in our own image." Karl Barth (1886-1968), who is credited with challenging the traditional interpretation of the *Imago Dei* contributed much to this relational view as after the image of the Trinity.[14] The image that God is a community of love and that God created humans to image the community of divine love in concrete historical setting has so much to offer us to value human life, community,

14 Karl Barth, *Church Dogmatics III/1*, trans. J. W. Edwards, O. Bussey, and Harold Knight, ed. G. W. Bromiley and T. F. Torrance (Edinburgh: T&T Clark, 1958), 152, cited in, Megan K. DeFranza, *Sex Difference in Christian Theology: Male, Female, and Intersex in the Image of God* (Grand Rapids, Michigan: William B. Eerdmans Publishing Company, 2015), 3.

male and female, young and old in an era where human society is losing the value of human life and the responsibility toward one another. This image however does not overrule or negate the functional and the structural view of the image of God, instead, it enhances and precedes the other two and directs them under the divine principle of love. In this sense, God's image of love, unity in differences, relational bond and of the subsequent spiritual and moral responsibility toward human lives and the rest of creation can help direct individuals and communities to confront and overcome forces that threaten to destroy the image of God in us.

3.3. God as Liberator and Humans as Co-Liberators

The Bible clearly portrays God as the liberator of the oppressed and the enslaved. Right from the Old Testament to the New Testament times, we see God actively engaged in the liberative acts; we see the God of the Bible on the side of the poor and the victims of various injustices and evils. Humans then, as created in and bearing the image of the liberating God, should take our divine mark of the loving and liberating God by becoming or participating in God's liberating activities here and now. While it is often tempting to address issues and give responses from the narrow perspective of the Christians in any consultations or seminars organized from and within the church and seminary environment, let us also be reminded to check ourselves and see (especially here) that the evil of human trafficking in the region is not confined to the tribal Christians alone but to all peoples, races, ethnic groups, communities, tribes, families and individuals living in the region, affecting everyone and every life. Hence, I wish that people of diverse faiths living in the region and in different social, political, economic and occupational levels should consult, unite and pool each one's spiritual and religious resources to combat this issue. To be blunt, each of us from different faith communities should be able to ground our stance on our own faith as basis that upholds the idea of the divine as the liberator and protector of the oppressed and then be inspired to become one with our God as co-liberators for those that are suffering and in pain. Each of us, if we profess to be children of God, we should take this god-given responsibility to become advocates, care-givers and healers of those that are ailing in the society.

3.4. Church's Prophetic Ministry among the Victims

The church in the NEI should review its calling, mission and ministry in the context of the evils prevalent in the society. The church as a believing and praxis community founded upon its Saviour – our Lord Jesus Christ, should critically re-examine its role and responsibility toward the evil of human trafficking in its neighbourhood and in the region. The church as an agency of God's reign should see that it not only focuses its ministerial attention upon the preaching of the Word on its pulpit on Sundays with the emphasis upon the salvation of the individual soul but on the holistic nurture of its congregation, the larger community and the society. It must address the evils that are affecting its members and the surrounding. Not just verbally addressing but doing something concrete and visible. Do our churches in the region have their ministry and programs that address and help the victims of trafficking?

Considering the fact that the most vulnerable group of people in the face of human trafficking are children, it is to be realized that the church should focus its service upon children and their families. One way of reaching out to the children and keeping them safe is through its ministry toward families. The local church is created by God for purpose of worshipping Him, to give sound biblical teachings, to protect the church from false teachings; to train/ disciple; to care for the believers and to equip them for ministry in their homes, community and in the world[15] (2 Timothy 4:1; Titus 2:1, 15; 1 Timothy 4; Acts 4:35; 1 Timothy 5; James 1:27; James 2:15 and Ephesians 4:12). The biblical image of families shows us that religious education was importantly centred in the home where parents and elders become the religious teachers. This interaction helped produce a family unity that made it possible

---

15 P. Scott, "Theological Foundations for Developing a Life-Changing Family Ministry," in *https://www.takejesushome.com/who-we-are/what-we-believe-2/* (20th September 2017).

to pass on values from parents to children and from generation to another (Psalm 78:4).[16] However, today, we see a huge shift in the responsibilities of the family. Most of the functions that were provided for in the biblical home are now operated outside the home. Throughout the Bible especially in the Old Testament we find God being the Father/Mother to the fatherless/motherless.[17] God's relationship is clearly pictured as a loving and caring parent to the children.[18] In addition we also find in the New Testament, God's serious concern for the children in the ministry of our Lord Jesus Christ. It is in this sound biblical directive that the church need to seriously reflect upon its ministry toward families – parenting and nurturing wholesome and responsible children. The church can help parents become godly parents in the holistic nurture and protection of children against the forces of evil such as human trafficking.

Though it might sound downright presumptuous on my part, the fact is, tribal churches in the region are lagging way behind as far as God's holistic mission is concerned. We are still unashamedly or guiltlessly floating in our self-righteousness and limiting the scope of God's liberative ministry that is entrusted to us. At the least, even if we cannot (due to various constraints) independently organize or set up full-fledged ministries, we could very well team up with other churches, organizations and bodies that minister toward and among the trafficked victims. For instance, in the region we have several NGOs, Civil and private agencies and programs that are working and helping human trafficking victims. Some of the notable ones are listed below:

Miqlat Ministry (NBCC): An NBCC undertaking for the rehabilitation of girls beside other oppressed-based programs. It

---

16 Wayne E. Rickerson, *Getting Your Family Together* (California: Regal Press, 1977), 8.

17 Dan Brewster, *Child, Church and Mission*, Revised Edition (Penang, Malaysia: Compassion International, 2012), 26-31.

18 Jesudason Baskar, Jeyaraj, "Biblical Perspectives on Children and their Protection" *Child Theology – India 2006: Theological Consultation – Children at Risk, Viva India* (Viva Network: Together for Children, 2006), Draft Page.

works in co-ordination with Women Development Department, Nagaland.

Caritas India: Its focus is on children illiteracy, child labour, child sexual exploitation, distressed migration of boys and girls.

Shakti Vahini: Identifies delay in charge sheets and low rate of conviction which are its main areas of concern.

IMPULSE NGO Network (INGON) Meghalaya: 1999 registered Meghalaya Societies Registration Act of 1983. This organization was formed because of the absence of services for the protection of trafficked victims and lack of effective victim-friendly procedures to prevent HT. In the early 2000s HT was not even acknowledged as a social evil in NEI. Hasina Kharbhih is the founder.

Ujjawala: A comprehensive scheme to combat human trafficking initiated by the Global Organization for Life Development in 2009. Its centre is in Guwahati, Assam. It is funded by the Ministry of Women and Child Development, Government of India.

Nedan Foundation: A non-governmental organization that works in the area of human rights especially in the rural areas. It focuses upon children in risk situations such as child trafficking, child abuse, child marriages etc. In Assam, its centre is in Kokrajhar.

Reiterating what I have commented on the church's laid back attitude towards the problem of human trafficking, the churches in the region can redirect and expand the direction and scope of their mission and ministry amongst the really hurting ones in the society – the trafficked victims. It is here that a critical self-examination is required with regard to the church's preoccupation with ministering only amongst the healthy and wealthy. The church as the agent and servant of God's salvation should faithfully carry out her God-ordained responsibility in the ministry of caring, comforting, healing, hope and transformation of the whole person - physical, mental, emotional and spiritual. Serious questions confronting the church today are: why is the church leaving all the seriously needy work to the secular (both governmental and private) agencies and groups? Is it not primarily the duty of the church to go out there in the midst of all filth and chaos, search, rescue and save God's children and bring them home? Churches in the region should seriously ponder over these questions.

4. Tribal Christians and Traditional Values

For want of space and time, we will limit our attention to only two of the cultural values here and they are: Community Parenting and Work Culture (dignity of work). The writer strongly feels that they can be very beneficial in our attempt to combat the evil of human trafficking in our tribal region.

4.1. Community Parenting

Tribal Christians should reclaim the traditional value of community-care and protection toward its members. I say this with much conviction and with much belief in the potency of this value, in the context of the threat of human trafficking. The poor, the defenceless, women and children are the most vulnerable lot when it comes to human trafficking. In the olden days, for instance, we had what we can rightly call the idea of "Community Parenting" and its practice when it comes to children of one's community or village.[19] The tribal community in many matters is bound together under a sense of belongingness and a sense of common duty. Anyone and everyone can become (even without being officially entrusted), a guardian or step-in parent for the children in the neighbourhood. Children would feel safe and secure under the watchful eye of the elders in the vicinity of the village, the community or in the fields. No elder would neglect or ignore any child that is in need of help, protection or guidance. By reclaiming this value of community parenting, community members can once again become the sentinel of the influx of strangers and of suspicious individuals loitering around the village or locality and

19 Lovely Awomi James, "Nurturing Children in Sumi Naga Tradition," in Razouselie Lasetso, I. Toshi Jamir and Woba James, eds., *Nurturing Children in the Tribal Society of North East India: A Search for Values* (ETC, Jorhat: ILEMA, 2014), 45.

especially around young children. This sort of community space in the nurturance of children helps people to feel safe and feel part of the greater family. Besides, it provides space for everyone to act responsibly toward the welfare and safety of children and their growth in the community.[20] This priceless cultural value and practice can offer a great deal to fight against the threat of human trafficking.

4.2. Work Culture and Dignity in Work

Secondly, the work culture of the tribals needs to be re-affirmed urgently. The tribals of old were known as hard-working people, who ate out of their labour. They were neither idle nor did they live a life of beggary. They tilled the ground, sowed seeds, planted fruits, watered and pruned their crops, guarded their fields and gardens for the sustenance of the family the whole year round; they walked long distances, collected firewood and other food materials from the forests and jungles, ponds, rivers and streams; they chopped wood, carved wood and stones, spun cotton, wove colourful and beautiful shawls, kilts and scarves, wove beautiful baskets and so on. This work culture was imbibed in every individual from an early age and they were well-trained and well-prepared for their survival, for adequate sustenance and for a comfortable life. Each individual learned the concept of responsible living and the wisdom of working and eating; there was no need to force people to work for their own benefits. However, when we take our present tribal context, majority of our people especially the youngsters have a strong aversion to work. Nobody wants to work; everybody wants to eat, sleep and enjoy. Try suggesting 'work' to them and most of them would react negatively. Many of them are ashamed to work; they feel that working is beneath them and their superior image of the self! There is no sense of guilt or shame in freely eating and enjoying life without even lifting a finger to contribute. And to complain that joblessness is behind poverty and poverty behind human trafficking! Such is our tribal Christian culture today.

---

20 Ibid.

All scientific education, technological progress and globalized culture that they have acquired have pushed them far away from basic human (moral, spiritual and ethical) values. But, here a word of caution is necessary: that the young are not to be totally blamed. In fact, if anything, the larger measure of blame should go to the parents and elders for failing to holistically nurture the young ones with those life-affirming and life-sustaining values. The Bible and our tribal culture both have rich resources to transform our life situations yet we ignore both and are thus on the way to self-destruction. Hence, before we completely lose our children to the evils of the world, it is imperative for the tribal Christians to reclaim some of those rich cultural values to heal and save our people.

5. Theological Education: Does It Address Human Trafficking?

The history of theological education goes back to the Biblical times and with God as the author and the perfect teacher or educator. It has gone through numerous shifts in the growth and development so also in its emphasis in accordance to the signs of the times down through the centuries. Today, we have come far and to a great extent in attempting to shape and develop our theological curricula around issues that are prevalent and urgent for our time. Yet, despite its apparent zealous attempts, it is still very strongly engrossed in the traditional western and mainland Indian philosophies and structure of theological education. Major portion of our curricula is centred on the study of old theological formulations and subjects that have very little or no relevance at all for our lives, our struggles and our times.

Yes, we say that we have subjects that deal with women, dalit, tribal, subaltern, HIV/AIDS, disability, human sexuality and the like (most of which are recent addition), but the truth is, we simply study them as side dishes, as peripheral issues for the sake of showcasing the view that we are being very relevant and practical with the urgent realities of our time. We need to admit that we still give more emphasis upon those outdated theologies, theologians and doctrines. As far as the reality of human trafficking is concerned, we give a feathery touch upon it within those minor subjects like women, children and HIV/AIDS. The questions before us are these: when are we going to seriously address this giant of an evil called 'Human Trafficking' in our theological education? What can our theological education offer to fight against human trafficking? When are we going to develop or formulate a sound theological teaching that can truly address and help eradicate human trafficking? We can only hope to achieve our goal only when we take the totality of our people's living realities – worldview, culture, religion, socio-economic and political realities and their day-to-day experiences, their aspirations and their visions, their hope and the like. This should be seriously considered and acted upon in our theological education and formulations to make the Word of God 'real', 'coherent' and 'meaningful'.

6. Critical Evaluation and Conclusion

Factors that promote risk of human trafficking are multiform. Poverty, unemployment, lack of access to adequate food, absence of schemes for family allowances, lack of compulsory education facilities, large families, illiterate and ignorant parents, traditional mentality or attitude etc.[21] While addressing human trafficking, it is necessary to also look into the root causes that leave the children vulnerable to become easy victims of human trafficking. It is foolish on anyone's part to even imagine that we can tackle human trafficking by simply putting up laws and strategies against it without first addressing and mending the brokenness that is deep within the systems and structures of our society and our nation. One of the severe factors that is behind the rising tide of human trafficking in the region is without a doubt economic poverty and therefore, it is crucial that the people – policy-makers, leaders, and citizens alike should take this issue more seriously and work for the eradication of mass poverty of the region.

21 S. C. Joshi, *Child Labour: Issues, Challenges and Laws* (New Delhi: Akansha Publishing House, 2006), 18-29.

As far as the potentiality and prospects of the region for economic growth is concerned, North East India is considered to be very potent. It has very rich biodiversity, mineral potential (oil, natural gas, coal, limestone, graphite, quartzite etc.,) and forest resources. Consider some of the rich potentialities of the region: About 80% of the total hydropower potential in the country can be said to be present in the region. Arunachal Pradesh alone has 30% of the total available in the country. More than 10% of India's requirement of forest products are said to have been met by the region. As far as human development is concerned (especially with regard to economic, education and health), the region is said to be faring quite well than most of the other Indian states. Human and natural resources necessary for infrastructures development are very much available except that they require the presence and operation of proper laws and order. The North East zone, as per the classification of India's bio-geographic zone (which is divided into 12 zones and out of which 2 of them are in the NE),[22] is considered to be the richest zones in the country in biodiversity. The region is also called the 'Hotspot' of biodiversity.[23] As per the report prepared by the KPMG[24] and FICCI[25] for the developmental prospects of NEI, following areas are earmarked – tourism, energy, small scale industry, infrastructure, education, and environment. It also takes up

22 The 12 biogeographic zones are: 1. Trans Himalayas 2. West Himalayas 3. Eastern Himalayas 4. North East India 5. The Indian Desert 6. Semi-arid Zone 7. Gangetic Plain 8. Western Ghats 9. Deccan Peninsula 10. Indian Coasts 11. Andaman and Nicobar Island and 12. Lakshadweep Island. Of these, the Eastern Himalayas that comprise of Arunachal Pradesh and the North East India zone comprised of all other NE states, are in the NEI.

23 Pratap Jyoti Handique, "Biodiversity in North-East India," in Sujit Deka, ed., *North-East India: Geo-environmental Issues* (Guwahati: EBH Publishers, 2008), 140, 143.

24 It stands for Klynveld Peat Marwick Goerdeler and is the third largest accounting firm in the world, with its headquarters in Netherlands, established in 1897. It provides advisory services in accounting, consulting, tax and legal, finance and assurance.

25 It stands for Federation of Indian Chambers of Commerce and Industry. It was established in 1927 and is the largest and oldest apex business organisation in India.

the question as to "why the region could not spend the earmarked money [the central sector fund for the year 2014-15 which amounts to INR 48,000 crore unspent and sitting idle], and use expertise from various institutions to prepare an array of doable projects?"[26]

Some of the obvious factors that hinder the possible work of economic development in the region include:

a. Suspicion of the tribals toward change and development
b. Uncontrolled influx of migrants and their control over businesses and markets
c. The huge socio-economic gap between the populations
d. Mixed and uncertain attitude toward tourism
e. Insurgency or Indigenous Militancy
f. It is a shame for our region to be labelled 'de-industralized' and "economically a century behind"[27] by survey and research but that is the sheer truth. Lack of connectivity, resource-industry connections and market accessibility all contribute to hinder the region's potential for growth and sustainable development.
g. Tribal/Ethnic Conflicts
h. Corrupt and Poor Governance of leaders
i. Negligence of the Central Government
j. Lack of Infrastructure

At the close of the paper, the writer would like to call the attention of all the participants and readers here to some of those few insights highlighted and proposed for the objective of concerted effort in theologically responding to the evil of human trafficking in the region:

a. That God is on the side of the victims.
b. That the Bible is very serious about the punishment for the slave traders and traffickers.

---

26 "Emerging North-East India: Economically and Socially Inclusive Development Strategies," in *https://www.kpmg.com/IN/en/Issues AndInsights/ArticlesPublications/Documents/KPMG-FICCI-North-East-India-2015.pdf, 6* (Accessed 7th November 2017).

27 N. Bhupendro Singh, "Globalization and North East India: Challenges and Opportunities" in *www.nits.ac.in/departments/humanities/new_hum/social_scanner/3.doc*, 15 (Accessed 10th September 2017).

c. That the Bible strongly condemns human trafficking (Slave Trade).
d. That the Bible entreats the release of one's slaves from slavery to brotherhood and sisterhood in Christian families.
e. That Jesus is the Liberator, the Good News for those enslaved.
f. That there is a necessity to reclaim the theological anthropology based on the *Imago Dei*.
g. That God is the Liberator and humans are therefore Co-Liberators with God.
h. That the Church's prophetic ministry is among the victims.
i. That tribal Christians should reclaim our rich life-affirming and life-sustaining traditional values.
j. That our theological education should adequately address the serious issue of human trafficking in the region.

Allow me to close with what the Labour Minister of Bhutan, Lyonpo Dorji Wangdi said with regard to eradicating Human Trafficking which is worthy of note: that neither policies, laws, political nor socio-economic measures can ever be comprehensive or a total solution to such problems. He thus stated, "The key to more comprehensive and sustainable solution to end child labour [through human trafficking] lies in the hands of families, communities, the private sector, civil society, children and the youth themselves."[28] And to that I also add Church – God-ordained community of the faithful, which is empowered by God, the author of life, to go forth and give healing and hope to those suffering. Let us all (irrespective of our temporal differences) be re-rooted in God to reach out to embrace, to love, to respect and to protect lives. For, without God - our creator, our beginning and our end, there can be no real liberation and salvation.

---

28 "Child Labour Finds Its Way into Bhutan," in *thebhutanese.bt* (Accessed 10th November 2017).

8

De-Coding Human Trafficking in A Post-De-Globalizing World Through the Prism of Christian Social Ethics

John Mohan Razu

I

Positing the Past—LPG

I grew up during the Cold-war era, wherein the left-right binary was relatively simple and easily be comprehended. To be precise, one block that adhered to liberal democracy and free-market economics, while the other, gave much larger role to the State the right to regulate the economic sphere. The Cold War ended in 1989-90, resulting in the disintegration of USSR and the collapse of Berlin Wall. As a consequence, those who towed the line of democracy and free-market liberalism affirmed that global capitalism is the only system as the most successful and the other system based socialistic principles could not be sustained and thus failed. Both the binaries are enmeshed with economic imperatives and bound to have sociological and political implications. So, it is important to recognize this factor, rather than just pointing to black-white assessments of the Cold-War including the others that ensued. The Western block of Europe lead by the United States professed democracy and free-market liberalism and the Eastern-bloc of Europe led by USSR advocated state as the custodian and regulator pushed their views hardly and remained as two powerful blocs reign the world. Both deferred diametrically from their ideological and political orientations. In the melee, the philosophy free-market capitalism survived.

Early 1990s has been one of defining moments in the life of India and many developing countries of the world. For the protagonists of free market economics, it is a triumphant beginning because of global capitalism via Liberalization, Privatization and Globalization (LPG) which became a categorical imperative, a universal norm and an absolute ideology for almost all the nations and peoples of the world. Global capitalism as an ideology, a credo and a doctrine has captured the imagination of many minds and swept across the borders of nation-states with its "claims" and "promises" "progress," "prosperity" and "development". It also claimed that it would usher "win-win" situation to all and wipe-out "win-loss" equation. In sum, corporate capitalism via neo-liberal principles of LPG has been considered as TINA (there is no alternative). Many fell to its promises and claims thinking that capitalism had triumphed and considered it as the dominant ideology and shall reign forever. As against this position there are some who out rightly defied and initiated alternatives such as Joseph Stigletz, Paul Krugman and David C. Korten[1] who have

1 Paul Krugman won the Nobel Prize for Economics for the year 2008 for his analysis of trade patterns and location of economic activity 'Traditional trade involved exchange of goods that countries were good at producing rice from Chine, wheat from India, cotton from Egypt, wine from France.' For Krugman, today's trade no longer works like this. Trade is now dominated by a few countries that are similar to one another and often countries import goods similar to those they export. Krugman explained thus: countries (and companies) become more and more efficient at producing their merchandise as they sell more and more and at less cost to themselves and the buyers. This enables countries to exchange similar products. Cities grow, Krugman pointed out, because industries provide jobs and people want to work close to home. Haven't we known that for centuries? Gerald Aungier knew this in 1675 when he opened Bombay to free trade and what passed for industry in those times—One more timeless truth. Krugman while interrogating and critiquing the international trade and its mechanisms proved how international trade is monopolized by the capitalist bloc. He

challenged LPG, the global financial institutions (IMF and WB), trading arrangements (WTO), their processes, mechanisms and international instruments. A cursory look after 25 years of LPG in India and around the world would reveal that a vast majority of people—the poor and the vulnerable engaged in formal and informal sectors whose livelihood dependant on daily wages shows declining prospects of their future. The outcry and frustrations of billions of people who live on margins by selling their labour for meager wages are totally taken by surprise and live in the lurch. The proponents of LPG However, the present agrarian crisis warrants to understand the root causes that have unleashed realized that their slogans of LPG and TINA started cracking and by 2008 the corporate globalization propelled by global capitalism went totally berserk. The entire global economy faced the worst financial crises and lasted for several years. As a result, recession, unemployment and misery prevailed across the world. Those who subsisted on daily wages had to face multiple ramifications such as, migration, distress, violence, break-up of families, labour unrest and suicides.

The onslaught of LPG on poor and the vulnerable in particular has been horrendous. Hence, one should go to the roots to make an inquiry about the causes that contribute to the crises. The age of globalization generated prosperity for the rich and the transnational corporations. Never in the human history have we witnessed so much of wealth generated and at the same time we come across widening inequality within and between nations. There have been protests and demonstrations against capitalism and globalization and also G-7, IMF, WB and other transnational banks and corporations. The hype the globalizing forces created

---

has been consistently opposing the forces of globalization for many years. Joseph Stigletz who won the Nobel Prize for Economics a few years ago is a staunch critique of global capitalism and international financial institution, wrote a seminal book on *Globalization and its Discontents*. David Korten, yet another outstanding Economist who taught in Yale and served on big foundations for several years and eventually spent more years in Asia contributing to the third world economies and known to have authored many scholarly books.

eventually became a nightmare. The forces that propel the current fiasco need to be identified. Analysis should entail the changing contours of global economy and in the process pitching the actors and agencies to the foreground in general and the nature of ideological premises of politics.

II

Unfolding the Present—Post (De)-Globalization

Globalization is on the retreat and gradually ebbing out. The ethic and vocabulary of globalization was written in the liberal democracies of the West based on certain foundational assumptions: opening one economy and integrating with the global free-market economy to trade and capital would increase employment, GDP, GNP, foreign reserves, incomes, consumer choices and tastes and so, values and beliefs. It was also thought and believed that globalization would eventually become the universal exemplar and aspirational trend setter. The claims of globalization made a whole generation of politicians, scholars, trade economists, commentators and many from academia eventually got converted and thus became robust evangelists to the credo of globalization. The forces of globalization failed to live up to the expectations and many who subscribed to globalization had no other excuses and justifications to offer in the wake of series of failures the people across the globe faced and experienced.

The era of globalization has generated great prosperity for the capitalists and the transnational corporations. During this era, the flight of capital moved from place to place looking out for cheap labour, incentives and concessions; movement of labour and people across the borders surged and in that the elite class globally accrued huge profits; professional classes moved to different corners of the world for lucrative jobs. The process and mechanisms that the forces of globalization employed widened the inequality further stirring stiff resistance among those who were left behind from market mechanism in many pockets of the world. As a result, what happened to the discontented and those who have been the victims of globalization, turned to the nationalists and right-wing politicians for remedy and solace who in turn promised to impose controls on free trade, transnational transactions, multilateral trade, stringent immigration policies and monitoring labour and flight of money?

A new age of de-globalization has dawned and is on in full stride. It is gaining momentum and spreading across the world swiftly. Populists are taking over the governments as evidenced by the stunning victories of Modi, Trump and May. Populism is gaining momentum and acceptance is gradually spreading in other countries as well. The populists and right-wing conservatisms in India, USA, UK and other countries subscribing to populism have called for protectionist measures such as tightening their borders. Their move does imply—a clear indication sending signals that the open world order is breaking apart. The new age of de-globalization is set and is likely to continue. We would be witnessing many more reversals in the new age of de-globalization as the post-war order is under attack from both popular autocrats in the emerging powers and election of populist candidates in other countries as well. Apparently, the slogans that populists use: "Make in India" "UK for Brits", "First America" along with host of others indicating that protecting domestic industry and territorial borders from the refugees and migrants and sharing wealth within the country gains more appeal and positive signals from the electorates—all in the name of 'nationalism and patriotism'.

Post-globalization believes in the distribution of wealth within nations for the rich and does not want to share the wealth equitably to all the citizens and beyond its borders. Distribution of wealth within and between will have salutary effect of narrowing the income gap between individuals. But, by protecting its borders and restricting the free movement of people could widen the wealth gap between nations. By opening its borders and pushing for borderless and seamless world, the dictum that globalization pushed had faltered in 2008, that helped the conservatives to capitalize and thus mobilized vast sections of the victims of globalization against the forces of globalization. Since then majority of the countries show decline in freedom and increase in xenophobic conflicts spurting between communities positing intolerance.

These democracies propelled by populism, the ultra-fundamentalist and rightist leaning elements by and large invoke nationalism and patriotism as their weapons to lynch and suppress its citizens. For these ideologues and followings, the notions of global village, inter-dependency, freedom of expression and free movement of people, live and let live and mutual co-existence are anathemas and in its place populist slogans and narratives are being replaced. The world in which we live is moving in this direction—tightening of immigration laws, toughening border security, nullifying the major trade deals and withdrawing support for allies. The consequential effects will be detrimental as the global movement of goods, money and people are likely to slow down drastically hampering growth, development and progress.

Globalization in its twenty-five years has connected societies, erased the seams of the borders, promoted digital opportunities, opened up its economy to foreign capital and transfer of technology, shifts in science and knowledge boom and thus entering into higher levels of innovative areas leading the countries towards new world order. But, in the process many were way laid and left behind. As a consequence, the counter-narrative by those who have been pushed out by the market forces showed their anger and resistance against globalization across the world and became glaringly apparent and a reality. The quest to reinvent the ethic and vocabulary of de-globalization is now on the upsurge. What we are witnessing is the walls within nations, open resentment against trade and migration, rising parochial and protectionist attitudes surfacing starkly across the globe.

The contour of global political economy has changed drastically. Since the elections of the populists in major democracies such as India and the United States, the crony capitalists have become the major influencing actors. They are found behind a demagogue or charismatic leader of the corporate state. Trump and Modi have given to their respective countries inverted totalitarianism, a persona and a face, by unfolding totalitarianism proper it could be totalitarian theocracy in India and totalitarian neo-liberalism. From now on we will be associating with this type of politics called as totalitarian. Anything could be taken as their weapon to push their agenda of divisive politics. Behind the mask of populism the totalitarian regimes whip the emotions of the masses more towards their brands of "aggressive nationalism" and "pseudo-patriotism. This is how they want to hold on to power by pointing to something "invisible" as enemies. Unmasking, demythologizing and evolving counter-narratives should be pursued to demolish their dominant narratives.

The transition is from global neo-liberalism to "national neo-liberalism" show the inter-facing of business and the state. Since their elections we come across slogans "America First" and "Make in India". Their narratives continue to attract those who have been sidelined by the market forces. Both the Indian and American voters are thrilled with their narratives. The populist have already created ideological covers for the closer connections between capitalists and the state. The new emergent politico-economic global landscape would further escalate enormous conflicts and high-levels of risks in all facets of human endeavours. We have been witnessing in recent times the rise of populism as well as the end of globalism thereby leading to the dawn of post-globalization. One should capture the shifting trends of politics and also the changing nature of issues that the people confront in their day-to-day living and in the process see through the contours of the issues that the people face and confront in their day-to-day existence.

III

De-Coding Human Trafficking—The Dynamics

Trafficking of humans is not a recent phenomenon. It has been in existence since the time immemorial. As centuries and decades pass by, its form, essence, value, areas and modus operandi did undergo sea changes. However, the core of human trafficking remains the same. Unless and until we go deep into the subject matter, we may not understand the intricacies and complexities of human trafficking. Human trafficking has been one of the most successful **trades** that managed to survive despite all restrictions, surveillance and monitoring and in recent times maintains a dubious status as its worth reaching to several billions of dollars and thus regarded as an "industry" along with other trades like "drug trafficking". The driving force behind human trafficking is global capitalism which is premised on profit maximization.

Capitalism kept progressing from one phase to another over centuries, revolutionizing its modes of production and diversified its operations of extracting labour by exploiting humans such as labour, women and desires to maximize its profits. It is amazing the ways with which capitalism keeps innovating new ways and means in keeping its ways as human society progresses. Human trafficking is one form of capitalist exploitation. Nonetheless, capitalism has survived and managed to survive and going stronger as the capitalists use their capital investing in a number areas where the returns are colossal and so it is considered by its proponents and those who believe in capitalism as the most successful economic creed, political philosophy and ideological power house. So for many, it is the best innovative politico-economic creed that has brought about transformative changes in the human activities such as production, consumption and distribution without which nations and societies would perish. Precisely because of these reasons they say and claim that there is no other alternative and so it would stay. It survived and now remains as the most successful brand.

Capitalism has the tenacity to bounce back, be it globalization (corporate, financial, casino) or de-globalization of diverse shades and formats. Capitalism is the underpinning factor that triggers the process. Unregulated fundamentals of free market economics is going strong, and in that capitalism both (global) and (local) does play significant and decisive roles in the changing contours of political economy. The basic tenet and driving force of capitalism is the mechanisms being employed to multiply the capital invested. For that to materialize, capitalism does involve in innovative ways and processes. Everything is being construed as materiality and thus commoditized, including human body vis-à-vis labour, women, and human organs, enticing materials that satiate humans as needs and wants and cater to profits. For capitalism to grow and prosper human body and labour play the concomitant part and the most significant role.

At the same time capitalism sustains itself as the capitalists involve in innovation by spending huge amounts of money in billions on R & D (Research and Development). Capitalism believes in the surplus which is converted as profits and so labour as the years to come be made redundant and in its place robots will be introduced. Nevertheless, human trafficking in all formats is certainly one form of the most rewarding of the capitalists' enterprise that augments profits. Trafficking of humans for various purposes, primarily to make more money, is being carried out within and between countries and continents. Prior to embarking into the intricacies of human trafficking it is important to know what human trafficking is all about "Human trafficking is the trade of humans, most commonly for the purpose of forced labour, sexual slavery or commercial sexual exploitation for the trafficker or other. This may encompass providing a spouse in the context of forced marriage or the extraction of organs or tissues including-for surrogacy and ovary removal."[2] Trafficking of humans can take place within a country or transnationally.

Human trafficking is considered as a crime because it is heinous and willed against persons who have been forced into. It is a violation against the person because every individual is entwined with basic human rights to make individual decisions about their movement and jobs. No one has the right to curtail the movement and choices of an individual through coercion and intimidation for exploitative motifs. Exploiting in whatever forms and nature tantamount to intrusion of one's rights and freedom.

2 For more details See Wikipedia, the free encyclopaedia titled *Human Trafficking*.

According to the International Labour Organization (ILO) forced labour alone (one component of human trafficking) generated an estimated $150 billion in profits per annum as of 2014. In 2012, the ILO estimated that 21 million victims are trapped in modern-day slavery. Of, these 14.2 million (68 per cent) were exploited labour, 4.5 million (22 per cent) were sexually exploited and 2.2 million (10%) were exploited in state-imposed forced labour.[3] By now, the number, forms of exploitation and its magnitude of human trafficking would have reached alarming heights. Hence, trafficking of humans is considered to be one of the fastest-growing activities cutting across the nation-states and has acquired transnational character and is controlled and promoted by the criminal organizations.

Human trafficking involves human person(s) per se for diverse purposes in the forms of recruitment and transportation, transfer, harbouring or receipt of persons by employing threat or force or forms of coercion, of abduction, of fraud, of deception, of abuse of power or of taking advantage of vulnerability or of luring by paying or receiving payments or promising benefits to achieve the consent of a person having control over the other person solely for the purposes of exploitation in return of money. Exploitation include all forms such as sex workers or other forms of sexual exploitation, forced labour or services, slavery or practices similar to slavery, servitude or removal of organs. Exploitation is the core of human trafficking and it exhibits in all forms. There are many actors and agencies involved in trafficking of humans. There are also many types of human trafficking such as trafficking of children, sex trafficking, forced marriage, labour trafficking and trafficking for organ trade. Within each type the form, method, modus operandi and stakes vary from one to another. In all these, those who have been affected and thus become victims are the women and children. The reason being they are susceptible and become easy prey in a world of patriarchy and male chauvinism.

3 Ibid.

IV

Shocking Reality—Trafficked, Traded, Enslaved

Human trafficking has stupendously scaled upward and reached its zenith. As global capitalism keeps innovating news ways and forms of exploitation in its stride, it undergoes different phases. In correspondence to the changing scenario, trafficking of humans too in the process has undergone sea changes. Human trafficking is considered as an "organized racket" with a turnover of billions of dollars. We live in a world of global capitalism spearheaded by the de-globalizing forces. Despite the walls being built, securing territorial borders, stalling migration, tightening immigration policies and curbing the movement of people, human trafficking continues to grow and spread at alarming levels by devising new ways and mechanisms. Out of many types one type has been taken as a point of reference to prove the case under scrutiny. The following stories amply testify the gravity and intensity of trafficking of humans:

The first episode is all about Soni, a popular name and is resonant amongst the Adivasis. She is at an undisclosed location in Bihar, in hiding, fearing for her life; recuperating from the injuries that have been inflicted to her soul. As she narrates her story over the phone she breaks down. As a minor she came to Delhi and in stages passed through and stepped into a world totally unknown to her—a world of slavery. She was confined in a tiny house where unknown men set in motion a whole cycle of exploiting her body and also other young girls who stayed. Soni was 15 in 2010 when she along with four friends moved out from her village in Jharkhand and met an agent and then underwent a sale and transfer of ownership to an agency and then had to work as a maid in a home in Delhi. During this period she lost track of her friend. After six months a man came to see Soni, who introduced himself as one from the "office". He saw her and then left.

Couple of days later another agent came and took her to a new house. She found the residents of the second house treated her harshly when compared with the residents of the first house.

They gave her Rs. 10,000 which Sony took and kept in a safe place. The new house was tiny and surrounded by narrow lanes. Sony was made to sign papers she could not read which was written in English. She was subjected to a strange routine and had started—regular check-ups at a hospital such as blood tests and most importantly, strange injections. She did not understand why she needed those injections. There were other girls in that house living a secluded life. The curtains were always firmly drawn. The security guards kept moving from one end to another and it was also filled with agents, staff members and a caretaker and a woman from Jharkhand known as '*Didi*'. This was the routine—sleeping, waking up, cleaning and eating. If Soni wanted fish she would be served fish and people were 'good' to her, but she failed to understand and could hardly comprehend 'why.'[4]

Later she found out the reasons for 'why'. A girl whispered to Soni in the bathroom that a baby was growing in her womb. Since Soni did not hear the word 'baby' properly, nor may have come across the word, she somehow failed to understand what she said since she was just 15 or 16. After three months of regular hospital visits in a curtained vehicle, Soni was taken for an ultrasound. Once she came back she pestered the caretaker that asking — "*Kya hai didi? dikhaiya na*, dikhiya na'. And she was shown a photo of a very small child—"ekdum chota sa bachcha tha."[5] The news came as a rude shock to Soni as she was young and for her age she could not digest that since her emotional maturity was to the level of an adolescent. This is the rottenness of system in which the vulnerable women and girls undergo all kinds of exploitation because by the time they realize they are pregnant; it is too late for abortion. Soni swallowed the hard reality and managed to go through. The caretaker told her to adjust and be good. She stayed on for another three months—in all about six months. They took her for walks in a local park and sent her to buy

4 Pragya Singh in his Cover Story, "Cops Call It Forced Surrogacy," in *Outlook*, 22nd May 2017, pp. 2427. Names have been changed to protect real identities of those who became the victims of human trafficking.

5 Ibid.

vegetables. Those who tried to run away were caught and brought back and beaten. Soni used to get scared but somehow managed. She won their confidence and one day, during the wee hours, she slipped out and asked a taxi driver to take her to the station. She had the Rs.10, 000 and used it for her expenses to reach Ranchi.[6]

Back in her village Soni, pregnant, wandered alone in the forest, tried many times to commit suicide—either by hanging or pouring kerosene, but survived. "I knew there was a child inside me, but didn't know how to tell anybody, how to explain how it happened" she says. She was aware of the fact that those in her situation had ended their lives, however, a male friend finally arranged a doctor for abortion when the fetus was four months. Soni recalled many things, memories flashed back as the tears rolled down her eyes; despite her mother's cries and warning her, even at the bus stand, asking her not to leave for Delhi, "I didn't listen—*meri zidd thi*—I was set upon going. The agent was from my village so I believed him." she says. Her father filed an FIR when he found that she had gone and yet there was no police investigation. When she registered a case, she received threats to her life. "The agents tore up my FIR and threw it away." she says. She did not mention the pregnancy in the FIR — "My FIR was only about agents selling girls for Rs. 40,000— 50,000 per child, but the police did not probe even this. Nobody supported me." she says.[7]

From a sense of sheer isolation and helplessness, a sense of belongingness of living in a community started to develop within her. In the meantime, Soni met another girl from Jharkhand who told her of having given birth six times, until her body gave way. "She got Rs. 50,000 per child. It is such a sad thing. I believe her. Nobody can live with a lie thin or big. I cry so much. Why did this happen to me? Why does it happen to unmarried girls? I didn't love anybody" It came from her guts; from her inner resources of vitality coupled with gradual recovery and vague apprehension about the future, kept Soni silent in public. "Tell the police? What

6 Ibid.

7 Ibid.

will they do? They will only ridicule me and I'll never be able to marry. My parents will be defamed, that's all. What choice do I have? What can anybody do for me?"[8] These were the questions that we keep hearing from those young girls who have been the victims of human trafficking. The second story certainly overlaps with the first and there are a number of commonalities on the physical and social map—but this one has an eye-witness. Rashmi is about 20 years old and when she was 13 years old, the system pushed her out of her village on the Simdega plateau in southern Jharkhand, bordering Orissa. In September 2014, Rashmi escaped from seven years of domestic slavery. The placement agent, who had lured her to that city back in 2008, put her on a train back to Ranchi. Rashmi travelled another 100 km by bus, crossing jungle and river to reach a familiar territory—the town of Gumla where her own people live.[9] It was the house of her sister and brother-in-law. After arrival they took her to the Child Welfare Committee (CWC) office in Gumla since it concerns about a child—a tale that talks about the lost years of childhood that concerns Rashmi. CWC is the only government agency authorized to hear and record such testimonies. Unfortunately the officers were out on that day saying — "Our team was attending a UNICEF function in Ranchi … so we didn't meet Soni" says Targen Panna, CWC's Gumla chairperson.[10] However, Rashmi's story was flashed in the media and then an activist took her to Shashi Kant, an anti-trafficking activist who heads an organization of his Chik Baraik tribe and is a journalist for a district paper. Rashmi recorded on videotape what she witnessed in Delhi.[11]

It is called as — "Bachcha Bechne Waala kaam" in the words of Rashmi; meaning, baby-selling. It has become a racket that has evolved in the shadow-zones of modern life of global capitalism to cater to the growing demands of human wants. Baby-selling is only the last link in the chain. In human trafficking baby

---

8 Ibid.

9 Ibid., p. 27.

10 Ibid.

11 Ibid.

production is a necessary interim stage. The market fundamentals dictate as per the dictates of demand so the supply will have to concur with it. It also reveals the exploitative nature and practices of human trafficking that unfolds a typical form of slavery. The video conversation with Rashmi ranging five minutes is one of the rare testimonies of what was always suspected to have happened in Jharkhand, but has not come to the surface so starkly—how the Adivasi girls have been trafficked, then raped, compelled to conceive, and finally their children sold in the flourishing adoption of the black market—it is an assembly-line of organized cruelty depicting modern slavery.[12]

According to the activists the price of a child secured through forced conception ranges between Rs. 1-4 lakh. The price rises in accordance to the demand and desperation of those wanting a child. Further, the fluctuations also depend on the willingness and agreement of Adivasi women, the risk factors involved and the problems to be encountered while conception especially the cold chain logistics.[13] The episode cuts deep into the phenomenon that has many layers. Since it is highly organized it is difficult to pin down the roots. The traumatized women often do not want to talk for a number of reasons. Victims go through all sorts of vulnerabilities and so do not want to disclose what really happened to them. The stigma is too strong and thoughts and memories would last till their death. The testimony such as Rashmi's is so valuable and thus reveals that it's just the tip of the iceberg. Rashmi's story was later published as a report which states that an agent named Chayin Singh took Rashmi to Delhi to a placement agency in Moti Nagar office of Manpower Bureau, run by Naina Kumari, allegedly one of Jharkhand's three most notorious traffickers—occupied with a number of babies and pregnant women. On one of her visits she met four girls, two of them pregnant who explained everything to her. Rashmi recounted that "Girls who get pregnant, their children are kept in

---

12 Ibid.

13 Ibid.

the agency office and sold after they are around one year old." "The police should have investigated the allegations ... We keep hearing of such cases but the victims are poor tribal girls. They recant under pressure from agents,"[14] says Shasi Kant.

V

Evaluating Human Trafficking—Through the Prism of Christian Ethics

In the previous sections the two live testimonies narrated exposits horrifying experiences that they did undergo in phases—trafficked, traded, enslaved, raped and made to conceive babies for adoption. These two cases represent the larger, vulnerable segment of young girls and women being trafficked within and between national and global borders numbering thousands and millions of young girls. As a consequence, Adivasi young girls are turned into baby-making machines for Rs 1-4 lakh per child. It is now termed as an organized racket that depicts cruelty, vulgarity and incivility. Its turnover runs to many billion dollars carried out by illegal traders—but well-organized, clinically worked out, cold-blooded and amoral enterprise.

At the heart of human trafficking—the central core of it is indeed the idea that one can exert absolute control over the other including her body. The terms such as abuse and exploitation does go beyond human civility because the human body is considered in a capitalist world as a commodity. Ever since the body of women was commoditized for maximum returns vis-à-vis womb construed as a device and the fetus as its product. Global capitalism as it progresses has made women's womb for rent—for profiteering. The stories evoke greater scrutiny, analysis and evaluation. Before embarking on those, if we call our society as civilized and supposed to be living in a civilized world, we should not pretend and thus not offer flimsy excuses and justifications for human trafficking—it has been there and would continue and nothing can be done.

---

14 Ibid., 28.

Global capitalism has entered into baby production because huge profits are involved. Capitalism has been using women's body as means of exploitation and now 'renting the wombs' is its recent one and its modus operandi is premised on the fundamentals of the market. The demand for 'surrogacy' has grown and for that they need young women. The demand is growing and to meet the demand there should be enough supply. For this, there should be regular supply of young women prepared to 'rent their wombs'. We need to view the whole gamut of human trafficking within the emergent framework—a supply chain and assembly, which is highly organized, propelled by diverse means and methods. Adoption of children nowadays is a flourishing black market. The whole assembly-line of human trafficking is nothing but an organized cruelty. Those caught in the web of human trafficking not out of their choice to enter into, but are forced into it; their experiences have been horrendous and traumatic. It should be reiterated that most of them became victims against their will. Lured by the agents, the teens from marginalized sections have fallen prey due to their vulnerability as baby producing machines.

The questions that confront those who have been trafficked that haunt them all the time are: Why did this happen to me? Why does it happen to unmarried girls? They did not love anybody, had no friends. Why should god do this to them—have they done any harm to anyone? We see the depletion of their inner resources paving way for vague apprehension about their future. They are a selected lot and have no future. On a similar vein, Soni asked the following questions: — "Tell the police? What will they do? They will only ridicule me and I'll never be able to marry. My parents will be defamed, that's all. What choice do I have? What can anybody do for me?"[15] These questions amplify total devastation of their dreams and aspirations. For them, their whole life and future came to a grinding halt. Commodifications of bodies by the forces of capitalism for profits show that the modern phase of exploitation we have entered. Using the wombs of the Adivasis

15 Ibid., 27.

against their will and without their knowledge shows the total breakdown of laws and failures of enforcement agencies.

The basic tenet of capitalism is to maximize the returns by way of profits and to get it there, are no scruples. As pointed out by Siddharth Kara, the author of *Sex Trafficking: Inside the Modern World of Sex Slavery* states that "one woman or child is trafficked for the purpose of sexual exploitation every 60 seconds in the world."[16] He observed that sex slaves are invariably moved from poor areas and countries to richer areas and countries. The central argument of his book is that "the enormity and pervasiveness of sex trafficking is a direct result of the immense profits to be derived from selling... around the world. The structures of Western capitalism ... contribute greatly to the life destruction of lives this profitability entails."[17] Despite the UN Protocol to Prevent, Suppress and punish trafficking particularly women, define exploitation of trafficked persons for forced labour, slavery and other forms of sexual exploitation. Nonetheless, the existing legal framework to combat trafficking includes many along with related provisions, but somehow they fail to arrest the growing menace of human trafficking.

Human trafficking is the worst form of inhumanity inflicted against other humans who are susceptible. Over and above, sex trafficking and in that exploiting the womb of young women for surrogacy without their knowledge and consent is immoral. To substantiate, "Sex Trafficking, one of the ugliest contemporary actualizations of global capitalism because it was directly produced by the harmful inequalities spread by the process... deepening of rural poverty, increased economic disenfranchisement of the poor... erosion of real human freedoms across the developing world... sex trafficking requires and attack on the industry's immense profitability and a radical shift in the conduct..."[18] Profits accrued by exploiting the

16 Quoted by Divya Trivedi, in his article titled *A call for dignity* in "Frontline", November 13, 2015, p. 104.

17 Ibid.

18 Ibid., p. 105.

wombs of innocent young women ought to be brought under the prism of ethics—as Christians under the domain of Christian ethics. Therefore, all human actions as Christians ought to be brought under Christian ethical prisms. It is puzzling as well as anguishing as we read and hear the testimonies of two young Adivasi women who were trafficked, raped and forced to deliver babies. Conscious people are often puzzled by these episodes that they face and confront in the real world.

This is particularly true in our complex fast-changing world. We as Christians particularly those belonging to the tribal, Dalit and Adivasi communities are agonized over human trafficking in the face of violence and exploitation. Capitalism and other patriarchic tenets could offer all sorts of 'moral justifications', but certainly fails to offer any justifiable moral reasoning to human trafficking. Nonetheless, our age is plagued by so much uncertainty that we tend to forget that there has always been a gap between moral commitment and moral judgment. The basic questions that arise are: what are the implications of Christian faith for our actual moral judgments? What should be the Christian attitude toward sex trafficking?

Subjectively committed Christian must ask an objective question what he/she should do about his/her commitment in the wake of human trafficking. Both the subjectively committed Christians and objective questions that are asked ought to revolve around Jesus Christ as the norm in the Christian moral life—while making decisions and entering into action. Our claims and actions ought to invoke Jesus Christ as normative. Therefore, Jesus Christ is normative for a Christian's moral purpose whether convenient or whatever. He is the standard by which our decisions and actions are measured. He becomes the centre and content-filled symbol for our efforts to discern what God is enabling and requiring in the world we live in. Hence, our ethical framework seeks to relate the sphere of morality to God, by living and protecting God's moral order in such ways that-what God wants and how God in Christ commands us to live and lead our lives in particular moral ways so that the moral commands direct our actions to "humanize" life.

God in Jesus Christ came into this world to humanize and redeem this world from all sorts of bondages, so that all may be one and live in abundance. If this is the categorical imperative for us 'here and now', then it is mandatory that,

> If God's will is that of humanization, Christians ought to be doing what God does; that is, they ought to be engaged in humanizing activity. If the moral order created by God is an order of justice and love, the "What does the Lord require of you, but to do justice, love, mercy, and walk humbly with you God?" Theological ethics is necessarily involved in a process of theological interpretation of what occurs in experience and in history, since the vocation of the believer is to "respond to all actions upon him and to respond to God's action" in H. Richard Niebuhr's language, to be obedient to the command of God; in Barth's language, to endorse and coincide with God's humanizing activity; as Lehmann suggests, to be in accord with man's true tendencies and ends as God has created him to be, Thomaistic language.[19]

The wombs of the young women being converted as baby production chambers for profiteering ought to be interpreted in the light of specific Christian commitment that emanates from the uniqueness and centrality of Jesus the Christ to our faith and the normative principle for elucidating what God wills in the world we live. And so, for the Christians, the starting and ending point—the Alpha and Omega and also for all ethical evaluation Jesus Christ—the human and divine becomes the norm, the value and operative principle. While affirming the goodness of the created order, it is important to recognize the very fact that the world in which we live promote that goodness amongst fellow human beings, so that goodness will have to be nourished and sustained, transferring hope and love, freedom and trust.

As we witness the phenomenon of human trafficking—exploiting the womb of young women to amass money unfolds the gravity of the issue that warrants us to take position between

19 James M. Gustafson, *Christ and the Moral Life* (New York: Harper and Row, Publishers, 1968), p. 266.

justice and injustice, life-destroying and life-affirming forces. Experiences of young innocent Adivasi women portray the depths of inhumanity they meted out and in the process had faced all sorts of dreadful experiences that robbed their womanhood and dignity. More importantly, a question that emerges at this point as Christian(s) is: what I or we to do in a situation like this? We are talking about the pathos and agony of thousands and millions of young women who suffer and undergo all sorts of exploitation day-in and day-out. What should be the Christian response and how are we to reconcile with trafficking of humans which is diabolic and de-humanizing? When faced with situations like this we need to consider multiplicity of things that come in our ways such as means and end that are possible and defensible, between loyalties and commitments that we hold and between various moral principles that can be brought to bear on the situation. So, we are often baffled when surrounded by competing ethical principles that inhibit our decision-making process. For instance,

> To say that I will act to coincide with God's action—humanizing, or creating, sustaining, judging and redeeming—does not resolve the matters of choice. And if I admit that such theological interpretation as I engage in is inevitably unclear and inaccurate by virtue of my finiteness and various natural and wilful biases. I can rely even less on my Christ informed interpretation to answer my moral question. There are no simple religious or theological resolutions to moral choices; they almost always involve choices between things that are each of some value and each of some perversity. To choose one is not to another, and with that choice some possibilities are irrevocably lost and others are on the way to conditioning the course of my life and the events.[20]

The above quotation opens up the predicament and ambiguities we as humans go through while making decisions. The whole process is indeed complex and cumbersome For instance, in a situation like human trafficking "... the analyses

20 Ibid., 267-268.

and choices are human, made by finite creatures with various biases and perspectives, and as the effects of human agency they can never claim divine sanction unambiguously."[21] Therefore, in situations like this Jesus Christ becomes the norm of our ethical discernment. The normative principle that illumines and undergirds Christian ethics for making ethical decisions is none other than Jesus Christ. Invoking and illumining his words and deeds that personify God‘s infinite love to humanity that reflects loving care and compassion and goodness and love for humans to sustain and survive. In Christ we are thus mandated in obedience to love which requires in-principled love or love in dialectic with equity, fairness and justice manifesting relational responsibility to self and the neighbour that directs us to do in given ambiguous context–specificities.

The whole process zeroes down to "Christ gives insight and direction; he shows something of the way in which his disciples are to follow. He helps them to see what options are more in conformity with the human good as it is understood in and through God‘s work and disclosure in him. He helps them to see what choices about ends to be sought and means to be used are in accord with trust in the goodness of God who gives and sustains life, and who acts to redeem it."[22] As humans, our response to the commands of Jesus Christ ought to be responsive to the course of events that affects the humanity of fellow human-beings. The mores that are employed and used for evaluation is not something that an individual or a group has but more in tune to bring the oppressive forces under God‘s moral domain. In the process, it is to establish one's personhood integrated around those who have been the victims and what she is and means.

Christian discipleship calls for doing what Christ asked us to do. It pre-supposes what Christians ought to do by ways of responding, participating and showing solidarity with those who have been trafficked, enslaved, raped and used as machines and in the process have lost their humanity and personhood. The struggle

---

21 Ibid.

22 Ibid., 269-270.

by all means should be between the life affirming forces as against life-negating forces. "In other words, simply checking trafficking will not help as long as centres of exploitation exist. Acquisition of sex slaves primarily occurs in one of these five ways: deceit (false job promises), sale by family, abduction (least popular as it complicates trafficking), seduction or romance (marriage), or recruitment by former slaves (rarer),"[23] Kara says. Over and above, "in India, Dalits, tribals and other marginalized communities are extremely vulnerable to trafficking and constitute a large proportion of the bonded labour force."[24]

It is undoubtedly modern slavery and "... is the third biggest organized crime globally and a $10- billion industry."[25] According to Sunitha Krishnan who works on these issues says that "The process of trafficking destroys the body, mind and soul of a person and a corresponding support system has to be in place to take care of this damage."[26] It is paradoxical that after drug and arms, human trafficking is the third largest profitable in the world and in that Jharkhand happens to be the worst victim in India and in that the trafficked girls are impregnated and made to bear children. Sunitha Krishnan does use the soul of a person which M. M. Thomas calls it personhood. Personhood as normative principle ought to be taken more seriously in the case of those innocent productions for higher profits. As a consequence their personhood is being totally crushed, badly wounded and deeply hurt. Personhood is undoubtedly one of the key normative principles that acts as the axel around which other categories hangs on, such as human rights, human dignity, equality, equity and fraternity. Personhood touches upon the most inner self—the core of selves that each and every women reveres the most. It is theirs and they would not allow others to inflict pain or intrude into it.

---

23 Divya Trivedi, "A Call for Dignity," in *Frontline*, November 13, 2015, p. 105.

24 Ibid.

25 Ibid.

26 Ibid.

In such a vulgar and dehumanized scenario, the real alternative and our vocation ought to be humanization. It is unfortunate that this vocation has not been considered and thus negated. While on the other, the victims have been yearning for freedom and justice, and by their struggle they believe and hope to recover their lost humanity. Their humanity has been stolen. As Freire rightly articulates that "While the problem of humanization has always, from an axiological point of view, been humankind's central problem, it now takes on the character of an inescapable concern."[27] Hence, "Concern for humanization leads at once to the recognition of dehumanization, not only as an ontological possibility but as an historical reality."[28] In this context of human trafficking, humanization is indeed a realizable possibility. The reason being those young tribal women wanted to live and be fully human, but could not be realized. And so, their humanity by all means would have to be restored. Therefore, as pointed out by Immanuel Kant that human beings are to be treated as means and ends, and certainly not as means for one's ends.

27 Paulo Freire, *Pedagogy of the Oppressed* (London: Penguin Books, 1993), p. 25.

28 Ibid.

9

Restoration and Rehabilitation of Trafficked Victims
Pastoral Care Perspective

Arenla Longkumer

Introduction

Human trafficking or trafficking in person, as they are interchangeably used, is a major global concern. It poses as a dreadful reality in the contemporary world. Trafficking includes forced recruitment, transportation or harbouring of persons for the purposes of labour, prostitution, organ transplant, and smuggling of drugs and arms. Persons irrespective of age and gender may become victims of human trafficking. However, an alarming number of women and children from poor families become easy victims of trafficking due to absence of social protection, economic security and legal support.[1] The most common definition on human trafficking identifies trafficking in persons as:

> The recruitment, transportation, transfer, harbouring or receipt of persons, by means of the threat or use of force or

1 H. K. Mohajan and Siddhartha Sarkar, "Human Trafficking and Organized Crime in Asia," in *Gender, Trafficking and Migration: Are Women Really Empowered?* ed., Siddhartha Sarkar (Delhi: Manglam Publications, 2016), 221 (221-245).

> other forms of coercion, of abduction, of fraud, of deception, of the abuse of power or of a position of vulnerability, or of the giving or receiving of payments or benefits to achieve the consent of a person having control over another person, for the purpose of exploitation. Exploitation shall include, at a minimum, the exploitation of the prostitution of others or other forms of sexual exploitation, forced labour or services, slavery or practices similar to slavery, servitude or the removal of organs."[2]

This write up is an attempt to give an overview on human trafficking and its consequences. It tries to suggest a ministry towards restoration and rehabilitation of trafficked victims from a pastoral care perspective.

Consequences of Human Trafficking

Victims of trafficking suffer severe physical, psychological and social consequences due to the harsh treatments in the form of sexual abuse, physical violence, and emotional torture. Although, it is difficult to find out the exact consequences of trafficking on its victims due to its secretive nature, several researches are being conducted.[3] Victims of human trafficking commonly suffer the following consequences:

Physical – Human trafficking being exploitative in nature involves serious health-related consequences for the victims. Many victims are trafficked specifically for their physical characteristics and structures suitable for specific working conditions. As such their physical attributes are exploited resulting in many physical ailments. Due to the hazardous working conditions in which they labour, trafficked victims either fall sick, injure or die. Severe physical exploitation to

---

2 *Protocol on Prevention, Rescue, Repatriation and Rehabilitation of Trafficked & Migrant Child Labour* (Government of India, Ministry of Labour and Employment, 2008), 12.

3 Such as the *United Nations Office on Drugs and Crime, Toolkit to Combat Trafficking in Persons* (United nations Publications, Sale No. E. 06. V.11, cited by Joshua Nathan Aston, *Trafficking of Women and Children: Article 7 of the Rome Statute* (New Delhi: Oxford University Press, 2016), 40.

the extent of psychological damage often leads to developing suicidal tendencies in the victims. Women and children trafficked for the purposes of sexual exploitation undergo far more serious health related issues as they are treated violently and are forced into sexual activities. Their fear for life often manifests in psychosomatic symptoms. Many victims become vulnerable to HIV/AIDS and other sexually transmitted diseases.[4] Children who are forced to beg suffer from injuries that are purposefully inflicted upon them by the traffickers. Many of them are subjected to hunger and malnutrition and die of dehydration and other related illnesses.

Psychological – The experience of various abuses ultimately results in psychosomatic and psychological reactions. Such reactions manifest as fear, guilt, rage, sense of betrayal, distrust, helplessness, shock, suspicion and feeling lost. Trafficked women in particular, who are compelled into forceful sexual activities often endure persistent anxiety, fear and insecurity. Some of the commonly experienced psychological distresses include post-traumatic stress disorder; depression; anxiety disorder; disorientation; temper tantrums; paranoia; nightmares; memory loss; self-blame; extreme sadness; social isolation; hopelessness and helplessness; and suicidal tendencies and attempts.[5] Trafficked victims tend to develop behavioural problems such as becoming anti-social, aggressiveness, addiction, and sexualized behaviour.[6] Individuals with experiences of such negative emotions are likely to inflict self-harm or to commit suicide. However, there

4 C. Zimmerman et al., *Stolen Smiles: A Summary Report on the Physical and Psychological Health Consequences of Women and Adolescents Trafficked in Europe* (London: London School of Hygiene and Tropical medicine, 2006), cited by Joshua Nathan Aston, *Trafficking of Women and Children* …, 45.

5 Joshua Nathan Aston, *Trafficking of Women and Children: Article 7 of the Rome Statute* (New Delhi: Oxford University Press, 2016), 47.

6 C. Zimmerman, M. Hossain, and C. Watts, "Human Trafficking and Health: A Conceptual Model to Inform Policy, Intervention and Research," *Social Science and Medicine* 73/2 (2011): 327- 35, cited by Joshua Nathan Aston, *Trafficking of Women and Children …,* 46.

are indications of resilience and a quest for meaning among the victims that facilitated healing and adaptation despite the traumatic experiences.[7]

Social - Traffickers often lure the victims by offering job opportunities or fixing marriage alliance through friends or families. Gradually, not only the individual but the entire family or group gets trapped. Trafficked victims may also experience a sense of apathy/resignation, extreme forms of submissiveness to any authority, social maladaptations, and loss of personal autonomy.

Thus, human trafficking has become a serious concern for the modern society. It affects everyone and poses as a threat to human health as it includes various types of dreadful and communicable diseases. Human trafficking results in social disintegration and abuse of human rights. Most of all it results in serious psychological problems and mental problems among the victims. In short, human trafficking has become a present day threat to the very existence of human life.

Human Trafficking As A Traumatic Event

The definition of human trafficking clearly indicates that it is a remarkably traumatic experience. Irrespective of the intensity of the experience, every trafficked victim experiences some type of trauma. The experience of the trafficked victims is often considered as similar to that of post traumatic stress disorder (PTSD). PTSD is often used to describe a group of symptoms after being exposed to extreme traumatic stressors, mostly found among hostages, survivors and prisoners of wars. PTSD is frequently the individual's response to traumatic events. According to the Diagnostic and Statistical Manual of Mental Disorders - IV (DSM-IV),[8] an event is traumatic "if the person

---

7 Yakushko, Oksana, "Human Trafficking: A Review for Mental Health Professionals," *International Journal for the Advancement of Counselling* 31 (2009): 162 (158-167).

8 American Psychiatric Association, *Diagnostic and Statistical Manual of Mental Disorders*, 4th Edition (DSM-IV) (London: American Psychiatric Publishing, 1996).

experienced, witnessed, or was confronted with an event or events that involved actual threatened death or serious injury, or a threat to the physical integrity of self or others" and "the person's response involved intense fear, helplessness, or horror." It is then that the person fears the events, will be repeated, and avoids everything linked to the trauma.

The traumatic symptoms in trafficked victims are far more intense than those who undergo car accidents or natural disaster. Prolonged repeated trauma can occur only when the victim is in a state of captivity, unable to flee, and under the control of the perpetrator such as in prisons, concentration camps, and slave labour camps. Thus, the symptomatology of the trafficked victims, who are victims of inter-personal trauma, presents a more complex picture than the victims of single-incident trauma.[9] Victims of trafficking are exposed to situations in which traffickers were known to them, who, primarily very close and trusted persons subsequently exploited and took advantage of them. They are often family members, partners or friends. Thus, human trafficking represents a severe blow to basic trust and faith in people and their benevolence, a breach of dignity and fundamental human rights of the individual.

Human Trafficking and Complex Trauma

Trauma refers to any kind of physical or psychological stress that disrupts a person's stability. It is a life event that shatters the individual's view of the world as a safe, predictable and controllable place, in which the individual is incapable of cognitively and emotionally processing the existing coping mechanisms. Trauma occurs in different forms including physical injuries in accidents, abuses - physical, sexual or emotional, or any emotionally arousing encounters that leads to overwhelming psychological stress. The disturbing nature of trauma can make deep impact on individuals, destroy one's sense of trust and leave

9 Michael Korzinski, "Identifying and Treating Trauma in Victims of Trafficking and Exploitation," in T*rauma and Human Trafficking: Collection of Papers,* ed., Irene Koricanac (Belgrade: NGO ASTRA, 2013), 53.

individuals immobilized.[10] A traumatic event can be isolated, one-time event, or a continuous exposure to threatening events that the person perceives as difficult and menacing.

Irene Koricanac terms human trafficking as a complex trauma at least for two reasons. According to her, most individuals who become victims of trafficking have had severe childhood traumas. In the case of individuals with traumatic upbringing, the trafficking experience represents a trauma which cumulatively builds upon the earlier trauma that was not processed psychologically or dealt with. Secondly, victims of human trafficking undergo dramatic experiences. Therefore, victims of human trafficking experience complex trauma in which the traumatic experiences build on one another as they undergo particularly dramatic and unexpected events that can be equated to torture.[11] While the fact that everyone undergoes some kind of traumatic experience remains, the intensity of psychological reaction to trauma is proportional to the severity of experience that the person underwent. The traumatic experience of victims of human trafficking therefore points to an unprecedented situation that calls for an extraordinary concern and commitment from the human community including the Church. This calls for the Church to develop a specific ministry towards trafficked victims based on professional knowledge, moral commitment and pastoral skills.

Developing Caring Ministry For Trafficked Victims

Trafficking in persons is a complex phenomenon involving various issues ranging from deception and exploitation to abuses of various forms. The intensity of the damage caused by trafficking on individuals requires a long term recovery process of restoration, rehabilitation and reintegration. The process can include the ministry of intervention and prevention. Victims of trafficking commonly experience severe physical and psychological trauma

---

10 Gary R. Collins, *Christian Counselling: A Comprehensive Guide, 3rd Edition* (Nashville: Thomas Nelson, 2007), 763.

11 Irene Koricanac, ed., *Trauma and Human Trafficking: Collection of Papers* (Belgrade: NGO ASTRA, 2013), 23.

owing to the threats the traffickers use to exploit the victims. The ministry of pastoral care can help trafficked victims relief themselves of the anxiety, depression and fear and rebuilding their self-confidence. The experiences of various forms of abuses and the possibility of being infected with dreaded diseases such as HIV/AIDS make them vulnerable to stigmatization and social ostracizism. Hence, individuals and communities providing support to the victim needs to make a long-term commitment to help in this process.[12]

In the process of recovery and restoration, caregivers can help victims re-learn to trust others, and build healthy relationships. This would enhance their healing and growth. Many humanitarian and social agencies seek to restore and rehabilitate trafficked victims by providing basic necessities as well as fundamental legal and economic resources. Apart from the socio-economic support, addressing the psychological needs of the victims is of prime importance, which sadly seems to receive minimal attention and resources so far. It has also been observed that victims often indicated their wish to receive some type of counseling treatment and those who received counseling reported many positive outcomes such as a stronger sense of self and coping abilities to deal with the aftermath of their trafficking.[13]

Since most victims of trafficking live in fear, constituting a sense of safety from their perspective is important. Another important step is the reconstruction of the traumatic story. Many victims of human trafficking are reluctant to share their stories because of fear of rejection, or because of fear of retribution from their abusers. Gaining confidence and trust of the victims would enable them to open up about the horrific memories of abuse

12 Insights taken from *The Rehabilitation of Victims of Trafficking in Group Countries: A Study Conducted Pursuant to the Trafficking Victim Protection Reauthorization Act, 2005* (United States Agency for International Development, Office of Women in Development, 2007), 2-3.

13 Aron, L. Y., Zweig, J. M., & Newmark, L. S, "*Comprehensive Services for Survivors of Human Trafficking: Findings from Clients in three Communities* (Washington, D.C.: Urban Institute, 2006), cited by Yakushko Oksana," Human Trafficking ..., 161.

and trauma. Trafficked victims experiences situations and events that are beyond the ordinary human experiences because of the atrocities and abuses meted out to them. Hence, issues of trust and establishing rapport become significant in the helping process.

It is important for professionals in general and pastoral caregivers in particular to understand thoroughly the consequences that human trafficking leaves on a person's psyche. The frequent expressions of negative emotions, withdrawn, offensive, or maladaptive behaviour of the victims should be understood in the context of the trauma that they have undergone. Creating a safe and non-threatening environment is an essential task in helping the trafficked victims. The attitude of warmth, understanding, genuineness and acceptance of the caregivers can create an environment where victims of human trafficking undergoing betrayal and deception can begin to start rebuilding trust. It is only in such an environment that victims build a relationship of trust, accept themselves as persons with worth, and put their lives into perspectives.

Pastoral Caring Ministry Towards Trafficked Victims

The Church as a community that fosters fellowships, witness, and service must act diligently in devising contextually relevant ministerial methods of caring. The contemporary Church needs to carry its ministry in accordance with the fundamental principles of care in its commitment to the poor, the marginalized, the exploited, and the suffering ones. In the context of human trafficking, the trafficked victims and their immediate families and the community around are the suffering ones. Pastoral caring ministry can encompass all these groups of people. The Church as a caring community can ensure that pastoral caregivers and volunteers undergo professional training in order to address various human problems such as the effects of human trafficking, more adequately. The following approaches are suggested based on the fundamental functions of care in order to deal with the victims of human trafficking.[14]

---

14 These suggestions are proposed taking insights from Joseph George, "HIV-AIDS" as a Modern Crisis Experience: Challenges for Pastoral Care and

Restoring the Person: Instilling the Courage to Heal

Trafficked victims are broken and bruised people who are in need of physical, emotional, psychological and spiritual restoration. Pastoral caregivers can aim to restore trafficked victims who have undergone harsh treatments at the hands of the traffickers and have lost their selfhood by restoring them to wholeness and leading them to advance beyond the previous condition. The victim can be encouraged to integrate the different aspects of life and move to a higher spiritual or emotional level. The decision to heal from the trauma of trafficking is a powerful affirming choice that brings richness in life. Deep healing happens when one makes the choice to heal and change.[15] The task of the pastoral caregiver is to be open and attentive to the needs of the victims by deeply listening to the sighs and groans of the victims in distress. This calls for an emphasis on the power of the divine grace to heal both the inherent and the accidental deformities of human existence. This can include the recognition and a facilitation of the activity of a caring and loving God in the midst of human struggles. Presenting the God who heals as present in all of human struggles and who is able and willing to help in times of human crises including the traumas of human trafficking may enable the victims to gather courage and decide to take a step towards change and thus healing.

Rescue and Rehabilitation: Sustaining the Deprived

The Church and its various related agencies must move into action in order to engage with and share the burden of the suffering people. The complexities of the consequences of human trafficking calls for the Church and the community to develop a participatory method of caring where everyone gets involve and play their respective roles. The viciousness of the trafficking experience may hamper some victims to look beyond their trauma that can hamper their healing process. The experiences of betrayal and deception may push some victims to the extent of giving up on life

---

Counselling." *Bangalore Theological Forum XLV/2* (2013), 141-158.

15 Ellen Bass and Laura Davis, *The Courage to Heal: A Guide for Women Survivors of Child Sexual Abuse* (New York: Harper Perennial, 1992), 61.

and hope. In such context, even when healing seems impossible, pastoral caregiver can initiate to explore and discover strength and support from within and without and sustain the victim. In situations when restoring and leading the victim to a higher level seems not possible at least for the time being, one "stands by" and sustains them to continue and carry on with life with whatever strength and resource available. The sustaining ministry of the church does not end with some occasional charity or sympathy but should be expressed through a strong moral commitment to live and work with the victims of trafficking.

Prevention and Control: Guiding the Community

Human trafficking and exploitation deprives the victims of human dignity and worth for lifetime. The physical, sexual and psychological tortures leave irreversible scars in the mind of the victims. Prevention of such atrocious situations as human trafficking is an important task of the Church. Pastoral caregiver can enable trafficked victims to gather their resources from within and work towards their growth by helping them make right choices in life. While caring and educating them to safeguard from re-trafficking, it is equally important to create awareness among the mass about human trafficking and the destruction it leaves on human society. The church should work towards providing holistic education and personality development for children and vulnerable group of people so that they do not fall into the trap of human trafficking. Encouraging stronger family ties and reaffirming lives by recognizing individuals within the family as well as in the community as valuable and respectable members can prevent many individuals from giving in to the lures of traffickers and thus a victim. The church can also initiate the rich resources and wisdom that lie within the community and their cultural practices in addressing issues such as human trafficking.

Reintegration into the Community and Family: Reconciling the Alienated

The ministry of reconciling indicates helping alienated persons to establish or renew proper and fruitful relationship with God and fellow beings. Most cases of human trafficking happen in the context of interpersonal relationships. The deceptions and betrayals lead to broken relationships. Moreover, most victims either feel themselves responsible or are blamed by the family and community for giving in to the lures of trafficking. This creates a big gap between the victims and the family and the community. It can further lead to estrangement from God. The task of the church is to create harmonious relationships between people and ultimately between people and God. It is important to prepare the victims of trafficking who are in a way alienated from their families and from the communities they belong to, mend ways and be reintegrated to where they belong. This would enable them to live a life with dignity. The process of reconciliation and reintegration may be tedious and take a longer time. Pastoral caregiver can patiently facilitate reconciliation of the victims with their families and creatively search for means to bring them together in ways that are respectful.

Care and Protection: Nurturing the Victims to Grow

One of the most important tasks of the ministry of the church towards trafficked victims should be to extend care through the times of crisis. Victims of human trafficking undergoing the loss of selfhood and identity need the encouragement and support of caregivers in reclaiming their lives again. Pastoral caregivers can sensitively address the issues of different life stages and not just during a particular moment and journey together with the victims through their process of healing and growth. Trafficked victims whose trauma continues to follow them can be encouraged to leave their past attitude and limitations behind and to embrace new, potentially threatening, possibilities. Here the pastoral caregiver plays the roles of a comforter as well as a challenger.[16] Church and the caring community should create a victim friendly environment in which they would fully rediscover their potentialities and live life to its fullest.

16 Emmanuel Y. Lartey, *In Living Colour: An Intercultural Approach to Pastoral Care and Counselling* (London: Cassell, 1997), 40.

Acceptance and Identification: Empowering the Exploited

The Church as a faith community can accept and identify with those who are rejected and exploited. Such efforts to identify and share the struggles of the victims would result in empowering individuals and groups to deal with critical issues and concerns in life. The church can involve in advocacy work including the fight against stigmatization and discrimination of trafficked victims; addressing systems and policies to ensure better services for victims at the state and the national levels; support victim friendly legislations; and media advocacy to create awareness and change the perception of the society about the victims. Most victims of human trafficking have endured long periods of enforced and internalized helplessness or 'learned helplessness.' Accepting themselves as individuals with worth and gaining self-confidence is crucial for the victims of trafficking. It is in this context that the Church can facilitate in creating a victim friendly 'just world' for the victims of trafficking to fully enjoy their basic human rights as well as to utilize their potentialities to its fullest.

Within the context of a caring community, pastoral caregiver can help victims of trafficking in re-valuing their selves and personal characteristics and enable and motivate them to act and participate in the life of their communities. It is important to restore connection with victim's communities in their processes of healing and recovery. Victims of trafficking may eventually find connections with others who shared their experiences or get involved in organizations that fight trafficking. Such re-connections may result in empowering recovering individuals to make changes not only in their own lives but also to use their experiences for the healing of others.

Conclusion

The ministry of a caring community, the Church, will have an effective ministry of restoration and healing the victim of trafficking when they feel cared for, loved and accepted into the community. The devastating effect of human trafficking on individuals and the entire human society calls for a collective efforts of people from different walks of life. The Church can work in collaboration with different government and non governmental agencies, specialists and experts from different fields, social organizations and local bodies, and concerned individuals, in order to address the menace of human trafficking that threatens the very existence of human lives.

References

American Psychiatric Association. *Diagnostic and Statistical Manual of Mental Disorders*, 4th Edition (DSM-IV). London: American Psychiatric Publishing, 1996.

Aston, Joshua Nathan. *Trafficking of Women and Children: Article 7 of the Rome Statute.* New Delhi: Oxford University Press, 2016.

Bass, Ellen and Laura Davis. *The Courage to Heal: A Guide for Women Survivors of Child Sexual Abuse.* New York: Harper Perennial, 1992.

Clebsch, William A. and Charles R. Jaekle. *Pastoral Care in Historical Perspective.* New York: Harper & Row Publishers, 1967.

Collins, Gary R. *Christian Counselling: A Comprehensive Guide, 3rd Edition.* Nashville: Thomas Nelson, 2007.

George, Joseph. "HIV-AIDS" as a Modern Crisis Experience: Challenges for Pastoral Care and Counselling." *Bangalore Theological Forum XLV/2* (2013), 141-158.

Koricanac, Irene. Ed. *Trauma and Human Trafficking: Collection of Papers.* Belgrade: NGO ASTRA, 2013.

Korzinski, Michael. "Identifying and Treating Trauma in Victims of Trafficking and Exploitation." In *Trauma and Human Trafficking: Collection of Papers.* Ed. Irene Koricanac . Belgrade: NGO ASTRA, 2013.

Lartey, Emmanuel Y. In *Living Colour: An Intercultural Approach to Pastoral Care and Counselling*. London: Cassell, 1997.

Mohajan, H. K. and Siddhartha Sarkar. Eds. *Gender, Trafficking and Migration: Are Women Really Empowered?* Delhi: Manglam Publications, 2016.

Oksana, Yakushko. "Human Trafficking: A Review for Mental Health Professionals." *International Journal for the Advancement of Counselling 31* (2009), 158–167.

Protocol on Prevention, Rescue, Repatriation and Rehabilitation of Trafficked & Migrant Child Labour. Government of India, Ministry of Labour and Employment, 2008.

The Rehabilitation of Victims of Trafficking in Group Countries: A Study Conducted Pursuant to the Trafficking Victim Protection Reauthorization Act, 2005. United States Agency for International Development, Office of Women in Development, 2007.

United Nations Office on Drugs and Crime, Toolkit to Combat Trafficking in Persons. United Nations Publications, Sale No. E. 06. V. 11. In Joshua Nathan Aston, *Trafficking of Women and Children: Article 7 of the Rome Statute.* New Delhi: Oxford University Press, 2016.

Contributors

Miss Asha Sanchu
Director
Miqlat Ministry, NBBC
Kohima, Nagaland

Mr. T. Chubayanger
Project Officer
Directorate of Labour
Kohima, Nagaland

Miss Rossana Lyngdoh
Board Director
Impulse NGO Network
Shillong, Meghalaya

Mr. Tongpang L. Jamir
Advocate
Master Trainer
Nagaland State Legal Service Authority
Nagaland

Rev. Dr. A. Tali Ao
Associate Professor
CTC, Aolijen
Mokokchung, Nagaland

Dr. (Mrs.) Lovely Awomi James
Associate Professor
Eastern Theological College
Jorhat, Assam

Dr. Johan Mohan Razu
Professor of Social Ethics
Co-ordinator, Research Unit
Indian Social Institute (ISI)
Bangalore, Karnataka

Dr. (Mrs.) Arenla Longkumer
Associate Professor
CTC, Aolijen
Mokokchung, Nagaland

Bibliography

American Psychiatric Association, *Diagnostic and Statistical Manual of Mental Disorders*, 4th Edition (DSM-IV). London: American Psychiatric Publishing, 1996.

Anand, Nishant. *Women in India: The Problem of Missing Girl Child*. New Delhi: New Century Publications, 2016.

Ao, A. Tali, ed. *Voices against Domestic Violence: Biblical, Theological and Sociocultural Appraisal of the Experiences of the Oppressed Tribal, Children, Men and Women*. Mokokchung: CCPRA & Delhi: CWI, 2016.

Aron, L. Y., Zweig, J. M., & Newmark, L. S. "*Comprehensive Services for Survivors of Human Trafficking: Findings from Clients in three Communities*. Washington, D. C.: Urban Institute, 2006.

Aronowitz, Alexis A. *Human Trafficking: A Reference Handbook* (Contemporary World Issues). Zimmerram, Yvonne C. *Other Dreams of Freedom: Religion, Sex and Human Trafficking*.

Aston, Joshua Nathan. *Trafficking of Women and Children: Article 7 of the Rome Statute*. New Delhi: Oxford University Press, 2016.

Barth, Karl. *Church Dogmatics III/1*, trans. J. W. Edwards, O. Bussey, and Harold Knight, ed. G. W. Bromiley and T. F. Torrance. Edinburgh: T&T Clark, 1958.

Bass, Ellen and Laura Davis. *The Courage to Heal: A Guide for Women Survivors of Child Sexual Abuse*. New York: Harper Perennial, 1992.

Batstone, David. *Not for Sale: The Return of the Global Salve Trade and How We Can Fight It*. New York: Harper Collins Publishers, 2010.

Brewster, Dan. *Child, Church and Mission*. Revised Edition. Penang, Malaysia: Compassion International, 2012.

Brueggemann, Walter. "The Book of Exodus: Introduction, Commentary, and Reflections." In Leander E. Keck, et al., eds., *The New Interpreter's Bible: General Articles & Introduction, Commentary, & Reflections for Each Book of the Bible Including the Apocryphal/Deuterocanonical Books in Twelve Volumes*, vol. I. Nashville: Abingdon Press, 1994), 855.

Choudhury, Jayant and Manoshi Das. "Combating Human Trafficking with the NGOs in North-Eastern States: Some Suggestive Roles." In Awadhesh Kumar Singh, Atul Pratap Singh and Parvez Ahmed Khan, eds., *Trafficking in Women and Children in India: Emerging Perspectives, Issues and Strategies*. New Delhi: Serials Publications.

Christa C. Foster Crawford and Glenn Miles, eds. *Finding Way Through the Traffick: Navigating the Complexities of A Christian Response to Sexual Exploitation and Trafficking*. Oxford: Regnum, 2017.

Collins, Gary R. *Christian Counselling: A Comprehensive Guide, 3rd Edition*. Nashville: Thomas Nelson, 2007.

Craghan, John F. "Exodus." In William R. Farmer, et al., eds., *The International Bible Commentary: An Ecumenical Commentary for the Twenty-First Century*. Bangalore: TPI, 1998, 2004.

DeFranza, Megan K. *Sex Difference in Christian Theology: Male, Female, and Intersex in the Image of God*. Grand Rapids, Michigan: William B. Eerdmans Publishing Company, 2015.

Devi, Elizabeth and Prateeti Barman. "Women in Conflict Situations and Human Rights Violations: Experiences from Northeast India." In Daisy Bora Talukdar, ed., *Gender, Peace and Development in North East India*. Guwahati: DVS Publishers, 2012.

Divya Trivedi, "A Call for Dignity." In *Frontline*, November 13, 2015, p. 104.

Elowsky, J. C. ed. *Ancient Christian Commentary on Scripture: New Testament*. Volume IVA *John 1-10*. Illinois: IVP, 2006.

Farr, Kathryn. *Sex Trafficking: The Global Market in Women and Children*. New York: Worth Publishers, 2005.

Freire, Paulo. *Pedagogy of the Oppressed*. London: Penguin Books, 1993.

George, Joseph. "'HIV-AIDS' as a Modern Crisis Experience: Challenges for Pastoral Care and Counselling." *Bangalore Theological Forum XLV/2* (2013), 141-158.

Gustafson, James M. *Christ and the Moral Life*. New York: Harper and Row, Publishers, 1968.

Handique, Pratap Jyoti. "Biodiversity in North-East India." In Sujit Deka, ed., *North-East India: Geo-environmental Issues*. **Guwahati: EBH Publishers, 2008.**

Hopkins, Ellen. *Traffick*.

Hunter, Zach. *Be the Change: Your Gide to Freeing Slaves and Changing the World*. Grand Rapids, Michigan: Zondervan, 2007.

James, Lovely Awomi. "Nurturing Children in Sumi Naga Tradition." In Razouselie Lasetso, I. Toshi Jamir and Woba James, eds., *Nurturing Children in the Tribal Society of North East India: A Search for Values*. Jorhat: ETC, ILEMA, 2014.

Jeyaraj, Jesudason Baskar. "Biblical Perspectives on Children and their Protection." *Child Theology – India 2006: Theological Consultation – Children at Risk, Viva India*. Viva Network: Together for Children, 2006.

Joshi, S. C. *Child Labour: Issues, Challenges and Laws*. New Delhi: Akansha Publishing House, 2006.

Kanaiya, Anita. "Human Trafficking - A Modern Day Slavery?" In *Drishtikone: Evangelical Perspective on Mission and Ethics* 3 (2012), 3.

Kara, Siddarth. *Sex Trafficking: Inside the Business of Modern Slavery*. New York: Columbia University Press, 2009.

Korićanac, Irena. "Human Trafficking, Trauma and Psychotherapy: Conclusions and Recommendations from the International Conference - Contemporary Psycho-Social Challenges in Combating Human Trafficking." In Irena Korićanac, ed., *Human Trafficking Trauma and Psychotherapy Collection of Paper.* Belgrade: ASTRA, 2013.

Korzinski, Michael. "Identifying and Treating Trauma in Victims of Trafficking and Exploitation." In *Trauma and Human Trafficking: Collection of Papers,* ed., Irene Koricanac. Belgrade: NGO ASTRA, 2013.

Kristen, Foot *Collaborating Against Human Trafficking.*

Lartey, Emmanuel Y. *In Living Colour: An Intercultural Approach to Pastoral Care and Counselling.* (London: Cassell, 1997).

Lloyd, Rachel. *Girls Like Us: Fighting for a World Where Girls are for Sale, and Activist Finds Her Calling and Heals Herself.* New York: Harper Collins, 2011.

Macias, Kathy. *Deliver Me from Evil.*

Malarek, Victor. *The Natashas: The Horrific Inside Story of Slavery, Rape, and Murder in the Global Sex Trade.* Arcade Publishing, 2004.

Mathew, S. P. *Temple-Criticism in Mark's Gospel: The Economic Role of the Jerusalem Temple During the First Century CE.* Delhi: ISPCK, 1999. pp. 72-75.

Miles, Glenn and Christa Crawford. *Stopping the Traffick: A Christian Response to Sexual Exploitation and Trafficking.* Oxford: Regnum Books International, 2014.

Mohajan, H. K. and Siddhartha Sarkar. "Human Trafficking and Organized Crime in Asia." In *Gender, Trafficking and Migration: Are Women Really Empowered?* ed., Siddhartha Sarkar. Delhi: Manglam Publications, 2016. pp. 221-245

Muthunayagom, Daniel Jones. "Election in Relation to Mission of the Church in a Religiously Pluralistic Context: An Old Testament Perspective." *Bangalore Theological Forum* XLI/1 (June 2009).

Oksana, Yakushko. "Human Trafficking: A Review for Mental Health Professionals." *International Journal for the Advancement of Counselling 31* (2009), 158-167.

Osumi, Yuichi. "Deuteronomy." In William R. Farmer, et al., eds., *The International Bible Commentary: An Ecumenical Commentary for the Twenty-First Century*. Bangalore: TPI, 1998, 2004.

Protocol on Prevention, Rescue, Repatriation and Rehabilitation of Trafficked & Migrant Child Labour. Government of India, Ministry of Labour and Employment, 2008.

Raju, T. Swami. *Christian Theological Response: Contemporary Contextual Concerns*. New Delhi: CWI, 2014.

Rickerson, Wayne E. *Getting Your Family Together*. California: Regal Press, 1977.

Romaniuk, K. "'I am the Resurrection and the Life' (Jn 11:25)." *Concilium* 10/6 (1970), 70.

Rylaarsdam, J. Coert. "The Book of Exodus: Introduction and Exegesis." In *The Interpreter's Bible*, vol. I, ed. G. Arthur Buttrick. New York: Abingdon, 1952.

Sadananda, D. R. *The Johannine Exegesis of God: An Exploration into the Johannine Understanding of God*. Berlin/New York: Walter de Gruyter, 2004.

Seth, Roger. "Joseph, Human Trafficking Survivor." In *Drishtikone: Evangelical Perspective on Mission and Ethics* 3 (2012), 8-11.

Shelly, Louise. *Human Trafficking: A Global Perspective: A Global Perspective*. Cambridge: CUP, 2010.

Singh, Pragya. "Cops Call It Forced Surrogacy." In *Outlook*, 22nd May 2017, pp. 2427.

Skinner, E. Benjamin. *A Crime so Monstrous*.

Swartley, Willard M. "Slavery." In Joel B. Green, et al., eds. *Dictionary of Scripture and Ethics*. Grand Rapids, Michigan: Backer Academic, 2011. pp. 736-737.

Swartley, Willard M. *Slavery, Sabbath, War and Women: Case Issues in Biblical Interpretation*. Scottdale, Pennsylvania: Herald Press, 1983.

The Rehabilitation of Victims of Trafficking in Group Countries: A Study Conducted Pursuant to the Trafficking Victim Protection Reauthorization Act, 2005. United States Agency for International Development, Office of Women in Development, 2007.

Thompson, M. M. "The Living Father," *Semia* 85 (1999), 26.

United Nations Office on Drugs and Crime, Toolkit to Combat Trafficking in Persons. United Nations Publications, Sale No. E. 06. V. 11.

Venzke, Molly. *Caged No More*. Trafficking Hope, 2011.

Wenham, G. J. *Genesis 1-15*, WBC, vol. I. Dallas, Texas: Word Books, 1987.

Zimmerman, C., et al. *Stolen Smiles: A Summary Report on the Physical and Psychological Health Consequences of Women and Adolescents Trafficked in Europe.* London: London School of Hygiene and Tropical medicine, 2006.

Zimmerman, C., M. Hossain, and C. Watts. "Human Trafficking and Health: A Conceptual Model to Inform Policy, Intervention and Research." *Social Science and Medicine* 73/2 (2011), 327-35.

Webliography

"Child Labour Finds Its Way into Bhutan," in *thebhutanese.bt* (Accessed 10th November 2017).

"Child Rights Violations and Trafficking Haunting North-East India," in *https://reliefweb.int/report/india/child-rights-violations-and-trafficking-haunting-north-east-india* (Accessed 9th Novenber 2017).

"Emerging North-East India: Economically and Socially Inclusive Development Strategies," in *https://www.kpmg.com/IN/en/IssuesAndInsights/ArticlesPublications/Documents/KPMG-FICCI-North-East-India-2015.pdf, 6* (Accessed 7th November 2017).

"Fight Against Child Trafficking: Challenges before the Media," in *https://www.unodc.org/pdf/india/shillong.../Fight_Against_Child_Trafficking.pdf* (Accessed 10th November 2017).

"On Human Trafficking: A Biblical Perspective," in *https://www.unodc.org/documents/treaties/UNTOC/Publications/TOC%20Convention/TOCebook-e.pdf* (Accessed 7th Nov 2017).

"Remember our Slavery: Jesus and Human Trafficking," in *http://www.scrib.com* (Accessed 8th November 2017).

N. Bhupendro Singh, "Globalization and North East India: Challenges and Opportunities" in *www.nits.ac.in/departments/humanities/new_hum/social_scanner/3.doc*, 15, (Accessed 10th September 2017).

P. Scott, "Theological Foundations for Developing a Life-Changing Family Ministry," in *https://www.takejesushome.com/who-we-are/what-we-believe-2/* (20th September 2017).

Union Minister of State for Home, Hansraj Gangaram Ahir states, "According to information collected and compiled by the National Crime Records Bureau from all the states and Union territories in 2015, 6,877 cases of human trafficking were reported. Of this, 1,539 cases were reported from the Northeastern States." Out of these 1,539 cases, 1,494 cases were registered from Assam. Cf. "Assam Tops Human Trafficking List," The Telegraph (Thursday, November 9, 2017, in *https://www.google.co.in/search?dcr=0&source=hp&ei=RdoDWvulcTmvgTuiKsw&q=human+trafficking+in+north+east+india&oq=Human+Trafficking+in+North+&gs_i=psy-ab.1.0.0l10.1870.13237.0.15610.29.27.1.0.0.0.319.3919.0j19j2j1.22.0....0...1.1.64.psy-ab..6.23.3937...0i131k1j0i10k1.0NBe-FrHxu1M* (Accessed 9th November 2017).

Waters, Julie. "The Intersection of Law, Theology, and Human Trafficking in The Narrative of Joseph: Linking the Past to the Present." In *Second Annual Interdisciplinary Conference on Human Trafficking,* 2010. 8, *http://digitalcommons.unl.edu/humtrafconf2/8.* (Accessed on 16/11/2017).